As I See It: From a Blind Man's Perspective

Revised and Expanded Edition

by

Robert Theodore Branco

ISBN: 1492349674

ISBN-13: 978-1492349679

Table of Contents

Note

The first edition of this book, which bore the same title, was published by AuthorHouse in 2007. Since that time, Bob Branco has written several more articles on blindness and on issues and problems facing the blind, most of which are included in this second edition of his book. Some of the articles included here were originally published in his own magazine, *The Consumer Vision Magazine*, between 2006 and 2013.

This second edition of *As I See It* was edited by **Leonore H. Dvorkin**, of Denver, Colorado. She also assisted with updating and adding to some of the information included here.

David Dvorkin did all the technical work required for the book's publication in e–book and print. He also designed the cover.

David and Leonore are both much–published authors, with more than 20 books and over 50 articles and essays to their credit.

For full information regarding their books, their other writings, and the editing and publishing services that they provide other authors, please see their websites. At the bottom of each of their home pages is a partial list of the authors whose books they have edited and produced thus far. Several of their clients are blind.

David Dvorkin: www.dvorkin.com

Leonore H. Dvorkin: www.leonoredvorkin.com

September 2013

About the Author

Robert Theodore Branco is a lifelong resident of New Bedford, Massachusetts. Legally blind since birth, Robert attended sight–saving classes in the public school system until his parents learned about Perkins School for the Blind, in Watertown, Massachusetts, 65 miles from his home. He spent eight years at Perkins, graduating from high school in June of 1977. His autobiographical book *My Home Away from Home: Life at Perkins School for the Blind* (2013) details those significant and formative years.

After graduating from Perkins, Robert went on to attend Bristol Community College and then the University of Massachusetts Dartmouth. He studied Business Administration at Bristol College, earning an Associate's degree, and then Finance at UMass, earning a Bachelor's degree.

Robert's work experience has been quite varied. He has been a health benefits counselor, a customer service representative, the manager of an automotive parts department, and the receptionist at a construction company.

For many years, he was Commissioner of Branco Softball, a slow pitch softball league; in that position, he was a blind man running an organization with over 200 sighted participants. He also hosted a support group for the visually impaired from 1999 through 2008. He still runs a bowling league for the visually impaired and otherwise disabled.

Currently, Robert serves on the Massachusetts Commission for the Blind's regional Consumer Advisory Council in his area. He also hosts trivia events at housing, day care, and senior facilities.

He is the publisher of *The Consumer Vision Magazine,* which is read in more than half of U.S. states and on three other continents. For details, see **www.consumervisionmagazine.com** In addition, he writes a weekly op–ed column for *Matilda Ziegler Magazine for the Blind*, which is a paid position.

He has taken dictation from another blind author, Jalil ("Jay") Mortazavi, to create a Word file of Mr. Mortazavi's forthcoming book, *From Iran to America: Changes, Choices, and Challenges.* Leonore and David Dvorkin will be editing the book and arranging for its publication.

You can reach Bob by email at **branco182@verizon.net** or by phone at 508–994–4972.

His website is

http://www.dvorkin.com/robertbranco/

For information on other books that Bob has written, please see the end of this book.

Chapter 1
Explaining Limited Vision

In my younger days, I was able to see more than I do now. At one point I saw color, tall buildings, lighted signs, lines on a highway, underpasses, waves riding over the ocean, the outlines of other people, and a full moon. I took all the essential eye tests. I saw more eye charts than I can count, as doctors tried to figure out exactly what I could and could not see. I tried to read large print as a child, but even with a magnifier, it was very difficult to keep up with other students in the sight–saving class at my elementary school. Therefore, I learned Braille, although I could still see enough to walk around without assistance, except for crossing a busy street.

Indeed, I went through it all! I wish I had been paid one dollar every time I had to tell someone how many fingers they had showing. The whole thing was tedious and quite boring, to say the least. I knew what I could see and what I couldn't, but people were so curious to find out that I had to show them. Despite how I felt about continually demonstrating how much sight I had, it was probably necessary for me to do so in order to satisfy my parents, doctors, and teachers.

If I didn't explain this entire process in detail and simply told you that I had partial sight, you might assume that I had more sight than I actually did. Look at it this way. If you say that you can see the figure of the person standing in front of you, someone else might suppose that you could identify that person. If I tell you that I can see a lighted sign at night, you might presume that I can see all the lettering on it. That's why I need to explain that although I saw human shapes and lighted signs, I couldn't identify them very often.

When I first went to Perkins School for the Blind in the fifth grade, I developed a reputation that was hard for me to fathom or stomach. It was difficult for me to explain just how much I could see and how much I couldn't see. Therefore, some of the staff believed that I had more sight than I was letting on. After a while, I felt very uncomfortable and was even afraid of getting lost, because people believed I could find my own way back from someplace even when I couldn't.

One morning before school, I didn't get a chance to play with the other children because one of my housemothers decided to take me around the playground to identify the color of each boy's jacket. All I could actually do was try to guess the colors. If I didn't guess correctly, she would insist that I knew the color but that I didn't want to admit it. Can you imagine the humiliation I was feeling? Although I thought that what the housemother was asking me to do was completely ridiculous, I knew she was my elder, my superior, and my so–called mentor; therefore, I kept quiet and showed respect for what she was doing.

There was more such humiliation and mistreatment to come.

In the boys' cottage at Perkins, each boy had his own bath towel hanging on a hook in the bathroom; above the hook was the name of the boy who owned that particular towel. Each name was printed on a clothing label with indelible ink. However, one of the cottage staff decided to test me and my supposed level of vision. She asked me to print my name in big, black, bold letters with a crayon and place the paper above my hook. Now, picture this. I was the only boy in the entire cottage whose name was printed in crayon with large letters. How embarrassing that was for me! Once again, she was the authority figure, so I had to show respect for what she was doing.

When my paper was placed above my hook with the big, black, bold letters on it, I was asked by this staff member to walk back and forth from my bedroom to the bathroom so that she could see whether or not I could find my bath towel. I was the only one of 35 boys in the entire cottage with a gigantic, make–shift label for the whole world to see.

After my parents and others who knew me well intervened, these ridiculous attitudes concerning my vision stopped.

In those days, I hadn't yet been introduced to the white cane. Once I learned how to use it, especially when I got older and traveled around in my home town of New Bedford, Massachusetts, the cane became a part of me. What some people with partial vision do is try to live life without the cane, if they can; but at times, this can get them into trouble, either physically or by hearing others make snide remarks.

For example, I know a partially sighted woman who tried to do her grocery shopping without using a cane. To anyone else who bothered to look at her, she had all of her vision. Who would doubt it? She seemed as though she was getting around okay. She wasn't bumping into anything or feeling for the shelves with her hands. The problem began when the woman asked someone to help her read a label on a can of food. The person whom she asked became very sarcastic and implied that there was nothing wrong with her, that she should know how to read. If she had been carrying a blind person's cane, it would have identified her as someone with limited vision, as someone whom people should notice and be willing to assist as needed.

Up to now, I've been talking about how people often assume that those with partial vision have more vision than they really do. But sometimes we're told the opposite. Here's an example of that.

After I graduated from Perkins, I had mobility training in New Bedford. I learned how to cross streets, shop in stores, walk around college campuses, and take buses independently.

During one of my lessons, my instructor asked me to cross a main intersection without assistance. As I was crossing, my instructor noticed that I was trying to use my limited vision in order to see when the parallel traffic would start to move. Even though I saw the car move from the corner of my eye, my instructor insisted that I not use my vision, saying that I should rely solely on my hearing to listen for parallel traffic before I crossed the street. When a blind person is taught how to cross a street, he's told to listen for parallel traffic, which is the traffic on the street he's not crossing. Once that traffic goes, he can cross, as long as it's absolutely safe to do so.

During my twenties and thirties, my sight gradually deteriorated—so much so that presently I can hardly see anything. The doctors call it optic atrophy, and I've accepted it. Looking back, I'm grateful for what I was able to see when I saw it. At least I have those memories to recall and to share with others who care to ask about them.

Chapter 2
How the Blind Find Employment

For those of us who are out of work, finding a job is a job in itself. We're taught by guidance counselors, career counselors, or workshop leaders that we need to fill our days with résumé writing, phone calls, networking, and all other aspects of finding work if we're going to succeed. I learned many years ago that despite what these professionals expect us to do in order to find a job, blind people must work twice as hard as sighted people. After decades of experience, I've found that there aren't enough hours in a day for a blind person to keep up with the sighted when it comes to job searching. Many employers lack information about what a blind person can do in a particular job setting. This lack of understanding results in the blind being rejected more often than the sighted, even though the blind do exactly what's required when looking for work.

The question we have to ask ourselves is this: What does a blind job seeker have to do in order to be as successful as a sighted job seeker? If you take into account that a blind person does everything he has to do, with little or no results, then someone has to show employers how the blind can function on the job. Because it's usually difficult for blind individuals to convince employers of their skills, they must turn to agencies that support the blind. Someone has to sell the skills of a blind worker. I'm not speaking about all employers. There are some whom I'll speak about later in the chapter who are quite receptive to hiring the blind.

I've been unemployed several times in my life and have been on many job interviews. I believe I have a lot of confidence when being interviewed, and I'm sure I can answer the prospective boss's questions well. However, with blind employees comes adaptive technology, which helps them be as productive as their sighted co–workers. I've used such equipment while working at some of my jobs, but I don't know how it's manufactured or programmed. I'm a consumer, not the computer engineer who invented it. Many times I'm asked how the adaptive technology works, but I can only answer the question to a point. Therefore, I can safely say that not only does a blind person have to work twice as hard as a sighted person to find a job, but he also has to be able to talk like a computer engineer in order to satisfy the employer's curiosity about this equipment. At this point, the agencies have to step in and help out. Many computer companies that produce adaptive technology are contracted with agencies serving the blind, so agency reps know more about this equipment than either the employer or the employee.

Let me explain some of what I know about adaptive equipment and the main ways in which I use it.

Years ago, I worked in the customer service field, and my computer had a speech program which helped me navigate through all the customer screens so that I could check the status of orders to find out how much the customer owed. With this same technology, I'm also able to write letters and articles, using the same word processing programs that sighted people use. On another occasion, I worked as a switchboard operator for a very busy medical center. I obviously couldn't see which buttons were lit up on the board, so I used a light probe with a sensor. When you point the sensor toward light, the small radio–like device gives off a buzzing sound to let a blind person know where the light is.

When I talk about how a lot of employers don't understand what the blind can do, I speak with a lot of experience. It's true that several of my interviews were productive and full of quality, but I've met some very interesting employers who didn't use common sense when speaking to me. Prior to meeting me, they had never had to deal with a potential blind employee.

A year after I graduated from college, I interviewed for a job at a local newspaper as a telemarketer. Obviously, one of the most important things you need to know as a telemarketer is how to dial a telephone. If you can't dial a telephone, how can you consider being a telemarketer? Well, I guess the head of this company didn't see it that way. I went into his office and sat down for the interview. At the time, I was a 26–year–old college graduate, so I'd like to think that I had already proven that I had some degree of intelligence. I came to him in all sincerity to apply for the telemarketing job. I wasn't looking for laughs. I take life seriously when it needs to be taken seriously, and I save my laughs for pleasure times.

During the interview, the employer asked me how I could dial a telephone. At this point, I didn't care how much of a risk I'd be taking if I gave the man a sarcastic answer. It was obvious at this point that I didn't want this job. So I pointed out to the employer that I had called him in order to schedule the interview, and how could I have done that without dialing the phone? Was he next going to imply that I would need a helper to dial the numbers? Keep in mind that he was the president of a small business. Is it possible that he believed he would have to hire two people to do the job I wanted? Let me say what you probably already know. If I were sighted, the boss would not have asked me about the telephone. He would have skipped that question and gone on to other questions, the ones he should have asked.

Perhaps I should listen to a friend of mine who's also blind. He keeps telling me that there's a big difference between common sense and intelligence. He believes that many people with a lot of intelligence have very little common sense, and vice versa. So maybe I shouldn't talk about this guy's intellect—or mine, for that matter.

When it comes to dialing a phone, many sighted people take light for granted. My mother, God rest her soul, needed light every time she had to dial a telephone, and when there was little or no light, she would ask me to dial the phone for her, because she couldn't see. I'm the one who can't see, but my mother couldn't dial the phone unless she had a fairly strong light on.

As of this writing, I've been out of college for close to 30 years. So far, I've explained how tough it is for the blind to find work, so I'm probably giving the impression that I've been unemployed for most of my life after college. However, I have such a passion for work that I taught myself at a young age how to be very creative when it came to job–hunting, because the traditional methods weren't working for me.

Since graduation, I've had a total of eight jobs. In all eight cases, I was laid off for one reason or another. I was never fired from a job, nor did I ever quit a job. However, in only one case out of eight did I get the job the traditional way. The other jobs came as a result of whom I knew, the intervention of employment specialists, and advertising my skills in the newspaper and on the radio. My very first full–time job was as a customer service representative for a local office supply company. The only reason I got the job was because I asked my local newspaper to do a complete story about my job search in relation to my disability. The owner of the office supply company read the newspaper article and proceeded to call me in for an interview, and I was hired. So you see, when nothing else works, we blind folk have to be more resourceful in order to achieve our goals.

While it's hard for most blind people to find a job, there are certainly many successful blind people in the world. I point that out to encourage those employers with little or no knowledge about this subject, to help them understand how feasible it is to have blind people in the work force. The following is a list of jobs that several of my blind friends have or had.

1. I have a blind friend who works as a supervisor of a Braille program at an agency that supports visually impaired people in Massachusetts. He instructs his workers on a daily basis.

2. Another blind friend spent two decades as a grant writer for a local school department.

3. Someone else is a sports writer for a local newspaper. With adaptive technology on his computer, he's able to write and then email his work to his sports editor.

4. I also know a blind attorney, a blind college professor, a blind entrepreneur who sells adaptive technology, blind high school teachers, a blind veterans' counselor, a blind store greeter, etc.

So, given all the success that some blind people are fortunate enough to have, should the rest of us have to waste our time explaining how we dial a phone? We are the consumers; there are agencies getting paid with our tax dollars to support us. Let these agencies step in and work to promote the blind with all their energies.

Chapter 3
Hot Dogs, Anyone?

As a child, you soon learn that it's important to respect your elders. As an employee, it's imperative that you respect the boss. And in the military, you must obey commands given to you at all times. Respect is an important building block in the formation of a complete human being; one can only imagine what might happen to a person with no sense of it.

Although most people show proper respect and courtesy in society, I find that many more people are now standing up to their elders, bosses, and other superiors than they did in my days as a child. It's true that many of our superiors make mistakes, and those who have to look up to their superiors, if they have the nerve, will try to right a wrong by taking a variety of actions: anything from answering the superiors back to suing them for misrepresentation or for violating their underlings' rights.

I recall one very important aspect from my childhood concerning my interactions with my elders, my teachers, and anyone else who appeared to be superior to me. Despite some of their shortcomings, I had to respect them because of who they were. It didn't matter what they did or how they did it; they were considered to be right because they were the adults and I was the child.

During my years at Perkins, particularly during my younger years, I met several teachers and staff members who acted in an unreasonable manner at times, but I never challenged their way of thinking. One such person was my sixth grade teacher. For the purpose of protecting his identity, I'll call him Mr. Jones. First, though, let me say that I thought Mr. Jones was a terrific teacher. We learned our lessons well, and as far as I was concerned, we grew from our experiences in his classroom. We sharpened our math, English, and geography skills, and at times, Mr. Jones made studying a lot of fun. However, he had his faults.

I would like to tell you about one of Mr. Jones's blunders, only to prove just how unreasonable a superior can be. After you read what he did to his students during the incident I'm about to describe, ask yourself whether you think he did it to be mean or because he had his own warped sense of reasoning. Also, consider whether you feel he tried to put one over on us because we were blind, especially if he felt that our lack of sight made us weak and timid.

During my sixth–grade year at Perkins, we, along with four other classes, spent a week in May at the Cape Cod National Sea Shore. The purpose of this trip was to provide the youngsters with a new life dimension. It was a chance to learn a lot more about nature, have fun, and be a bit more self–sufficient than usual. Each of the five classes that went to Cape Cod was accompanied by its teachers. We all stayed in one of the Coast Guard stations. Downstairs, there was a living room, a big dining room, the girls' bedroom, and a small kitchen, where we did our cooking. Upstairs were bathrooms, the boys' bedroom, and the staff quarters. Each bedroom had approximately nine bunk beds to accommodate all the children on the trip. As for cooking, each class took turns making the meals.

Prior to the trip, the children needed to prepare for the responsibilities we would all be facing. Two months before we left for the Cape, Mr. Jones gave us cooking lessons. His students would decide what they wanted to eat, and we'd learn how to prepare the food.

One morning we talked about preparing hot dogs. We were only sixth graders, so it wasn't as if we were going to make gourmet meals, like the ones you see on television. When the class agreed to prepare hot dogs, Mr. Jones asked us what we wanted on them. At that point, I should have guessed that there was something odd about the timing of Mr. Jones's question. It was still several days before we were actually going to cook the hot dogs, so why was it so important for him to know days in advance what we intended to put on them?

Perhaps you're thinking that Mr. Jones needed time to buy the condiments, so he needed to know how much of everything to get. Wrong! Mr. Jones had no intention of trying to figure out how many condiments to buy for his class. He wanted to keep things simple for himself, or so we thought. He told us that we must all agree on the types of condiments we wanted on our hot dogs, if any. If one student disagreed with all the others—for example, if only one student wanted mustard on his hot dog—then we would all have to eat ours with mustard, or none of us would have a hot dog at all.

After Mr. Jones laid down the law about our hot dogs, which we were so looking forward to eating, he went from student to student, asking what each would prefer. Surprisingly, most of us wanted our hot dogs plain, except for one girl, Elizabeth. She told Mr. Jones and her classmates that she wanted ketchup. We felt intimidated by the fact that Mr. Jones was our superior. However, we felt that he was being totally obnoxious about Elizabeth's decision to have ketchup. Another girl, Joanne, begged Elizabeth not to ask for ketchup, because her request was costing us all a hot dog. Elizabeth was hard of hearing, so imagine Joanne looking directly into Elizabeth's face, pleading with her in an extremely clear, emotional, anguished manner, like some people do in soap operas. I don't know how unsettled Elizabeth felt by Mr. Jones, but I know she was wondering why the heck she should change her mind about what she wanted. It's a free country, after all, so why shouldn't she have her ketchup? For that matter, why couldn't Elizabeth bring a bottle of ketchup to the cooking class, put some on her hot dog, and enjoy it while the rest of us enjoyed ours without any ketchup? That's the adult way of doing things.

This was actually very ironic, because Mr. Jones and the other teachers had to prepare their classes for adult responsibilities. What kind of adult responsibility was he teaching us by offering this foolish ultimatum about a hot dog? Elizabeth was the only one who made sense, really, because she knew exactly what she wanted and didn't think it would be a big deal if she was allowed to put ketchup on her hot dog. Yet, instead of standing up to Mr. Jones and supporting Elizabeth, we as a class sat back and showed our fear and intimidation. Because Mr. Jones was our teacher, he had to be right. Therefore, we felt required to beg Elizabeth to act in accordance with the rest of us, so we would get our hot dogs.

If I had had just a little more nerve in those days, I probably would have taken some sort of action. I don't mean that I would have done anything as drastic as trying to sue Mr. Jones for being so totally off the wall, but I should have reported him to our principal or to my parents. Perhaps subconsciously, we as a class felt that reporting Mr. Jones to the principal wasn't going to get us very far. The principal might have been one of these hotshots who believed that all of her staff members were competent and reasonable at all times, and that their blind students shouldn't be taken seriously.

By the way, I remember that cooking class we attended, and those empty, toasted hot dog buns actually tasted quite delicious.

Chapter 4
Adaptive Technology for the Blind

When I was a child, all I really knew about my eyesight was that it wasn't normal. However, I tried to live life as fully as possible, as a totally sighted person would. I knew that I would probably never drive a car, but then again, I knew that lots of people with normal vision didn't drive, either. The first significant difference that I discovered about myself compared to someone with normal sight was that I couldn't read books or newspapers. I used to watch my parents read, while accepting the fact that I couldn't. On numerous occasions between the ages of four and seven, I was tested, either in the home or by my eye doctor, in order to determine what size print I could actually read. By the time I was in second grade, it became apparent that I needed some alternative to regular books. Print was not the answer, and there was no way I would be able to keep up with my classmates, even in a sight–saving class, and I was in a sight–saving class for several years at a local public school, years before I entered Perkins.

I heard about Braille prior to my school days, and I was told that it consisted of a lot of dots. Of course that was all I could understand about Braille at the time, because I had never used it. However, in September of 1965, at the beginning of my second year in the sight–saving class, I was introduced to my official private Braille tutor, who would visit the class for an hour a day for the purpose of teaching me Braille. I was the only student in the class who couldn't read any form of print from a story book, so I had exclusive, one–on–one instruction, while the rest of the class went about their day.

As I learned Braille, I realized that it was much more than a series of dots. It was a language for blind people. We could actually read books by this method, and it was quite neat to be able to follow along in class with the other students, who could read print. In the afternoon, our regular teacher would have us read a story. She would ask little Johnny or Sally to read, and I would follow the story with my Braille copy of the textbook. When it was my turn to read, I would read some text out loud while little Johnny and Sally kept up with me in their print textbooks.

As time went by, I learned Braille abbreviations, Braille math, and eventually computer symbols. Before I lost my vision, I created my own large–print filing system by writing as large as I needed in order to see it. However, as I gradually lost my sight during my twenties, I thanked God for my knowledge of Braille, because suddenly it became my entire world. I had to convert all my print files and index cards to Braille, so that I would still be somewhat independent—

something that would have been very difficult to accomplish otherwise. Even now, as technology for the blind has become so advanced, I can't tear myself away from Braille, because it was and still is so important in my life.

When I entered Perkins in the fifth grade, I learned about another tool that a blind person could use, a tool which eventually turned out to be just as valuable to me as Braille. I'm talking about the white cane. At the time I was introduced to it, I didn't think it was a way of life for the blind. I thought that the cane was used just to familiarize a blind person with his surroundings, and that once he knew his way, he didn't have to use it anymore in that situation. In the sixth grade, I took a few mobility lessons, because I had to learn a new part of the Perkins campus in preparation for junior high and high school. I used the cane during those lessons, but once I was promoted and actually went to junior high, I didn't need it. It seemed as though none of my blind friends at Perkins traveled around the campus with their white canes. To this day, that amazes me, because I never leave home without it. The cane is my life, now; but in school, I didn't use it unless I was on a mobility lesson. Otherwise, I would hang my white cane in a closet or in the schoolhouse cloakroom.

At times, I traveled off campus, learning to cross streets and identify different forms of sidewalks. I learned right away how important the white cane is, especially when crossing a street. Today there are laws on the books pertaining to a blind person with a white cane who's crossing a street, laws that drivers are required to respect.

After graduating from high school, I learned how to travel in my hometown using the white cane. I learned the bus system and many busy intersections. I also had to learn parts of two college campuses.

Before I lost my limited vision, I carried a pocket watch. I could never really see the numbers printed on the dial, but I could always tell time by looking at the two hands. At that time, some of my friends with less vision used Braille watches. I never wanted one, because I was always afraid it wouldn't work right once I opened up the cover to check the time. You see, in order to tell time with a Braille watch, a person has to feel the two hands on the watch. I was always afraid that I was going to move the hands, making the time incorrect from that point on, so I never bought a Braille watch. However, after I lost my vision, the talking watch was on the market, so I purchased one. Twenty years ago, talking watches needed to be special ordered from companies out of state, then delivered by FedEx or UPS for a lot of money. Now, for lack of a better term, these watches are a dime a dozen at many local stores. They are also sold online.

In my home, I rely on many adaptive products to help me be as independent as possible as a blind person. The talking scale calculates your weight to the tenth of a pound; or if you want to convert to kilograms, the scale allows you that option. I always joke with anyone who stops by and wants to weigh themselves; I tell them that their weight won't be a secret anymore, because the talking scale will let all of us know. If my guests still want to weigh themselves, then they obviously don't care whether other people know their weight or not. However, I must caution anyone who weighs 300 pounds or more to stay away from my scale. One day a friend of mine who weighs that much stepped on the scale, and suddenly it stopped talking. Someone had to repair it later.

I own a talking thermometer which measures both indoor and outdoor temperatures. There are also talking blood pressure machines, measuring tapes, dictionaries, Bibles, pedometers, alarm clocks, clinical thermometers, and trivia games. The small light probe was designed to let a blind user know when the lights are on. If you point it toward light, the device will buzz, letting you know where the light source is. It comes in very handy when you want to check whether you've turned off the lights before bedtime.

More recently, items as sophisticated as the color detector and the paper money identifier have come on the market. Although it's wonderful to have this type of technology available for blind people so that they can identify money and colors, the devices are still rather costly, as I will explain in more detail later in this book.

To assist me with newspaper articles and typewritten mail, I have a scanner which converts print to speech, so that I can keep up with most of my mail. I say "most," because the scanner will not read handwritten material. I think it would be very difficult to manufacture a scanner that reads handwriting, because there are millions of different handwriting styles.

Despite our struggles, we blind are blessed with more opportunities for independence than ever, and a lot of the credit goes to those who manufacture all the adaptive technology I just talked about.

Chapter 5
Bad Habits

Have you ever seen a blind person who rocks back and forth, pokes his eye with his finger, or says things that only he or she understands? These are some of the habits I came across at Perkins. I have to be very careful when I talk about who actually has these quirks, because it's possible that some sighted children develop them as well. However, I honestly don't know that many sighted children who continue to behave in this fashion as they grow up. At some point, most sighted children realize how bad such behavior may look to other people, so they stop it—due to urging from their parents, increased self–awareness, or both. It may also be true that some blind people who possess quirky behavior eventually realize how bad it looks, so they try to stop it as well. However, there are many blind people, from children to adults, who, for some reason, rock back and forth, poke their eyes, tap their feet, or say silly things without realizing how different their behavior is. They have practiced such behavior for most of their lives, so these habits have become ingrained as they've grown older. I have firsthand knowledge of this; that is,

I have several nervous habits of my own. They probably originated when I first learned to sit up, and most of the time, I'm not aware that I'm behaving in this fashion.

As I observed this rocking, eye–poking, and other behaviors at Perkins, I began to ask myself why blind people possess them more than anybody else. There has to be a logical explanation as to why I can sit at a dinner table with a blind person who rocks back and forth, while 10 sighted people at the same dinner table won't do that. Recently, I started researching why this happens, and I think I'm onto something. Before I continue, I will admit to you that I don't have much of a psychology background. While it's true that many people with such a background are challenged by others anyway, you are allowed to challenge me and my theory more than you might had I majored in psychology.

But here are my ideas.

I think there are two important things going on when a blind child learns to sit up and eventually walk. As the child develops, he begins to test his body. He may start to move around, experiment, and create comfortable motions for himself, like rocking. Is it possible that many sighted children develop the same way? Absolutely; but in time, the sighted, who see how other children learn to develop, begin to understand what is and is not appropriate behavior. A blind child can't see what other children are doing (or are being told not to do), so that limits a blind child's understanding of acceptable physical behavior.

Well, if this is true, you might ask, then when should the parents step in and teach a blind child what is and isn't appropriate? Why do the parents allow any of this to go on?

In most cases, the parents of blind children do what is necessary; they work hard to teach their children acceptable social behavior, just as the parents of sighted children do. However, there are some parents who regard their blind child as special, unique—and, in some cases, fragile. They may not even be aware that they're making a mistake in allowing their blind child to explore in any way he or she chooses, even in an inappropriate manner. Or perhaps some parents are simply afraid to confront a blind child the way they would confront a sighted child, fearing that the child will be emotionally damaged by being told to change his or her natural behavior.

Were my parents this way? No. I received my share of discipline and punishment the way the average child in my generation did. So if my parents did the right thing by me, why do I have some of the nervous habits I'm talking about? Maybe my subconscious was working overtime when I was a toddler, so by the time my parents tried to address these habits, they were tough to undo. Perhaps other good parents also addressed their blind children's awkward behaviors, but they waited a bit too long to do so. Who knows?

At the beginning of this chapter, I referred to how I've been in the company of blind people who seem to have their own code or language, where they may say things that only they understand. For example, can anyone tell me what a "mox" is? I know a blind person who invented that word and actually defined it to his satisfaction. It's supposed to be some sort of new creature in the animal kingdom. My point is that some blind children, without the use of vision, may be focusing more on their own imaginations. I know I did. By the way, I'm not saying that sighted children don't invent words, hoping they appear or will eventually appear in Webster's dictionary. But given that I spent most of my adolescent life with the blind, I feel that I really got to know what goes on in their minds.

Allow me to take the "mox" a step further. Although the kid who invented the word defined it the way he saw fit, there was another reason why he used that particular pronunciation, "mox." Just bear with me as I take you on a tour of his vivid imagination.

Once he invented a mox, he decided to invent the mox's counterpart, the "momomox," spelled and pronounced as you see it. Where did he get the word momomox? To us, it may appear peculiar, but to this boy, it was very simple. The boy remembered the sound of a sewing machine as it was being shut off. He heard the motor going fast (MOMOMOMOMO), and then it stopped, making what he perceived to be the sound of the letter X. Therefore, you have "MOMOMOMOMOX." For some reason, he carried that term with him through his early adolescent years, and perhaps beyond.

Now that I've given you my theory as to why some blind people rock, poke, tap, and use their vivid imaginations, I think we can all agree that some of this behavior doesn't look very nice in public. However, believe it or not, I've spoken with defenders of it. Several years ago, the issue of rocking came to the forefront among my circle of friends, because a blind girl who frequently went out to eat with us did it all the time. However, during discussions about this, and in our efforts to try to stop this girl from rocking in public, her adult foster mother condoned the girl's rocking, because she thought it soothed her, making her calmer and more relaxed.

Another friend of mine, who is something of a psychology wanna–be, believes that these behaviors originate in the mother's womb. But I have to ask those who defend rocking and eye– poking in public: Are you trying to rationalize this behavior for the benefit of us, the blind, or are you defending it for your own benefit, so that you can come up with a reason not to confront these individuals, in order not to hurt their feelings? Of the provider who thinks rocking soothes the mind, I would ask, "Would you rock in public to soothe your own mind?" And to the wanna–be psychologist, I would say, "You came from your mother's womb and you behave just fine. So I guess you're implying that the wombs of blind rockers' mothers are different. And if that sounds too far–fetched, then perhaps you mean that rocking and eye–poking are hereditary."

In closing, let me assure you that I'm fully aware that many blind people do not possess the behaviors I've described. They conduct themselves properly, as they should. However, perhaps you can relate to why I introduced the subject in this chapter. Perhaps you've also had the occasion to wonder why someone rocks or pokes. Again, feel free to challenge or disagree with my theories—while, at the same time, realizing the number of years I've spent surrounded by the blind. For eight years, I ate with, studied with, played with, and roomed with blind schoolmates at Perkins.

Chapter 6
Questions and Myths

Even though many people understand how a blind person does things, there are a lot of people who aren't as familiar with the issue as they should be. Very often, when people first meet a blind person and want to start a conversation, there are questions they ask that appear unreasonable. Although these questions seem unwarranted to the blind person, I'm certain that the people asking the questions don't see it that way. They really want to know the answers. At times, their inquiries are realistic, but sometimes the questions are totally bizarre.

For example, I have a blind friend who is the father of three small children, and he does lots of grocery shopping. One day, someone asked him if there are grocery stores exclusively for the blind. Let's try to understand the question and the person asking it. First of all, I believe that most individuals are reasonably intelligent and know that there aren't any such grocery stores. Did you personally ever wonder if the blind had their own supermarkets? I assume that even if you know nothing at all about blind people, about how they live, behave, and go about their day, you wouldn't be so oblivious to your surroundings that you would think that there are grocery stores specifically designed for blind shoppers only.

It's strange enough that someone would ask about grocery stores for the blind, probably knowing all along that there are no such things, but some people take it one step further. My blind friend, the one who does the shopping for his three children, was also asked if the meats have Braille labels. Again, I'm having a major problem believing that anyone of average intelligence would actually ask such a question.

Believe me when I say that the way a blind person shops is not the only issue that we're asked about. When others try to find out how we blind people live and behave, the questions asked of us and the comments directed at us can be a lot more personal. As I cite these examples, I must be very careful how I word them, out of respect for those of you reading this book.

Recently, a young blind woman was riding in a taxi when the driver asked if she was "fixed." Before I comment on the issue as it relates to blind women, I want to make it quite clear just how aware I am that it was none of the cab driver's business, no matter if the girl was blind or sighted. What right does a stranger have asking any woman if she could ever have children again? As for the blindness issue, it is assumed by many people that the blind can't raise a family; therefore, at some point in their lives, blind females are expected by some to have their fallopian tubes tied.

While I was in college, I had a professor who taught us our lessons well but overstepped his social boundaries outside of class. One day I was sitting in the college cafeteria with five girls when my professor arrived on the scene. He told me that, because of my blindness, I could succeed in making a physical move on any of these girls because I would have a good excuse. After all, it was supposed that if I touched a girl's breast, it would be considered an accident. After all, I'm blind, so I'm not supposed to know what I'd be doing. Let me assure my readers that if I'm in a personal relationship and if the feeling is mutual between both parties, I know exactly what I'm doing and why.

By the way, the professor called this "the Braille method."

A blind male was asked how he knows where to aim when going to the bathroom. I don't know how you aim, nor do I care to know. All I know is that I walk toward the latrine until my legs come in contact with it, and then I use good judgment and common sense.

Many blind people are asked how they're able to make love. Let me just say that there are several ways to answer that question, but I suppose it depends on whether we want to be wise guys. For those people with an inquiring mind, I can show proof of many blind parents raising their own children. If the curious person isn't satisfied with that, then I could tell him that it doesn't take two eyes to find your mate's private body parts.

Oh, it gets even better. Many years ago, a young blind college man was approached by a girl who offered to show him how to perform sexual acts. She said she wanted the blind man to have that experience just in case he went through his entire life without it. She obviously felt sorry for him, and figured he would never have a relationship because he's blind. I'm not going to describe how the man reacted to the girl's warped proposition. Let's just say that he's probably the biggest blind Casanova in the United States, and he thinks he may have fathered many children unknowingly. I'm not trying to exploit this man's romantic résumé, only to point out that the blind are capable of being passionate, loving, and romantic, and are quite successful at having relationships. I know many blind couples who've been married for years, and I also know couples where one of the partners is sighted and the other blind. A lot of these couples are raising families quite successfully.

One of the most common myths about blindness that I've heard over the years from a sighted person is that our remaining senses are sharper because we can't use the sense of sight. I will try to put this myth into perspective. It's not that the rest of our senses are sharper by nature as a result of our blindness. It's merely that we depend on our other senses more than we probably would if we could see.

Many blind people have enough mobility and independent living skills that they carry themselves just as the sighted do. As a blind man, I expect that result. Quite often, a sighted person will see me walking around in a building or on a college campus and remark that I don't look blind. At first, I took it as a compliment, because the person obviously meant that I was acting normally. However, even though I try my best to conduct myself as any sighted person would, let's analyze the statement. When someone says that I don't look blind, what does that really mean? How is a blind person *supposed* to look? If the person didn't think I was blind, based on my actions, then how was he expecting me to act? Was I expected to stumble, bump into walls, fall down several times and not know my left from my right? Is this the behavior that the commenter expects from the blind? I feel that a blind person should be expected to conduct himself normally, as someone with all of his faculties. Being blind doesn't mean that we have to act like stumbling, bumbling idiots in order for someone to know we're blind.

In 1985, I was working for a local construction company as a receptionist. Our office was on the first floor, and we were quite accessible to the general public. One day, my boss had to move his company to another building, which meant that we had to work on the second floor. During my first day on the job in the new building, I obviously had to learn about my new surroundings—which was no big deal, at least as far as I was concerned. Well, my boss saw it differently. He walked over to my desk with an affidavit. He asked me to sign it in order to release his company from any liability in case I fell down the stairs.

I refused to sign such an affidavit. If I fell, and if the company was to blame, I'd want them to be held responsible. Besides, sighted people have fallen down the stairs. Should we talk about their excuses? As it turned out, one of my sighted co-workers in that same company slipped on a banana peel and nearly fell down the stairs, and my boss probably figured that the co-worker could blame the company for that mishap. But because I'm blind, he figured that it would be my fault if I slipped on a banana peel that someone in the company had unknowingly left on the stairs.

When I refused to sign that affidavit, my boss insisted. He said he didn't want my family taking his company to the cleaners if something awful happened to me. I still said no. Eventually, the boss backed off, because his attorney advised him not to pursue the matter.

I'll conclude on this note: How many sighted people really take the time to look at the stairs as they walk down them? In my younger days, when I had more sight, I always looked straight ahead.

Yes, I've had my share of questions and comments about us blind folk, but I've grown to accept people's curiosity and move on.

Chapter 7
Paper Money and a Suggestion for Improving It

Note: This chapter includes most of what was in the chapter on paper money in the first edition of this book, some of what the author included in a later essay called "Reshaping Paper Currency for the Blind," and some interesting information that I found online regarding how many other countries have paper currency of varying sizes and colors. — Leonore Dvorkin, editor of *As I See It*

* * * * *

Over the years, during many discussions I've had about blind people, the subject of money has come up. Many sighted people want to know how the blind take care of their own money. The only way I can respond to this is by telling them what I do, because I know that we all take care of our money in different ways. For example, I always fold my $5 bills and keep the ones straight. If I happen to have larger bills in my wallet, I fold them as well, but I keep them separate from my folded fives, which are all folded around each other. With this system, I always know what I'm giving people when I pay for things. But obviously, as I'll discuss in more detail in a bit, the concern is about what I get back.

It's been suggested by some advocates for the blind that paper money should be made with Braille denominations. However, first of all, paper money is too thin to support Braille well; and in the second place, how many people would actually appreciate having brailled money? Contrary to what most people believe, only about 10 percent of the blind know Braille, and because of the way money is constantly circulated, the vast majority of those who end up holding the money won't care if it's brailled or not.

So here is the question I'd like to ask: What if it were possible to have different sizes of paper bills, just as we have different sized coins? Fives would be larger than ones, tens would be larger than fives, and so on. Obviously, our varying coin sizes benefit both the sighted and the blind. I imagine that having paper bills of varying sizes and colors would help not just the blind, but also sighted people who handle money.

In case you think that such a practice would be an unusual or even a weird one, I'd like to refer you to an online article from Bankrate.com, entitled "Changes to currency may help the blind." The article says that the U.S. is the *only country in the world* that prints all its bills in the same size and color. Almost every other nation on earth prints different denominations in different sizes, and only the U.S. and Switzerland do not designate the different denominations by varying the color. So why not institute these practices in the United States?

However, believe it or not, there are blind individuals, as well as some consumer groups, who object to the idea of producing different sizes of bills with the purpose of benefiting the blind. That is, they feel that to do so would be to give the blind special consideration, a consideration which many blind people don't want. However, if these same blind people who don't want special consideration would realize that having different sized bills—just like having different sized coins—would help protect them from scams and theft, wouldn't they perhaps change their minds on this issue?

During my life, I've collected money at many fundraisers, for I can make change as well as anyone else, and I know exactly how to organize money neatly. Someone had to watch my collection box, though, just in case a customer gave me back the wrong change.

It's true that I can ask people how much money they're handing me, and it's also true that if they're honest, they'll tell me. But what if I happen to have some dishonest customers? The organization putting on the fundraiser would be penalized, while some clever scoundrels would go home laughing about all the extra money they made because they took advantage of a blind person. However, if bills of different denominations were of different sizes, such cheating could not happen, and there would be no need for a sighted person to watch the collection box.

I have some comments to make to a certain consumer organization that is against different sizes of bills because it feels that if there are different sizes of bills, the blind are being treated uniquely, and thus are not equal to the sighted.

First: I respect this organization totally for its stance on equality between the blind and the sighted. I believe that the blind should compete equally with the sighted for jobs, that they should have the same educational opportunities as the sighted, and that they should be awarded housing on the same merits as the sighted. But as far as money is concerned, why would the blind be getting special treatment if they had different sizes of paper money? With different sized bills, both the blind and the sighted would be able to identify the different denominations better and faster. Besides, if we want to go along with this consumer organization's argument that the blind have survived all this time with the same paper money that the sighted have, then we can also say that the blind have survived with different sized coins, just as the sighted have.

Second, the consumer group I'm referring to believes in independence. So, isn't it true that if the blind could tell which bills they had without asking someone, they would be more independent? Often, a blind person must ask a waitress, a cashier, a ticket vendor, or others who make change exactly what he's getting back. Sighted people don't have to ask; they already know, because they can see the money.

Finally, what about a situation in which someone tries to take advantage of a blind person when making change? Obviously, this can happen just about any time cash is being exchanged between a sighted person and a blind person, and not just at a fundraiser. A few years ago, I was robbed of $13 because a girl in my neighborhood told me she was giving me $15 back in change for a $20 bill, when in fact she gave me two ones. Obviously, I couldn't tell the difference between what I wanted and what I got. All bills feel the same to me. However, if bills were different sizes, I would have known what she was doing and would have caught her in the act.

I don't think that the blind are equal to the sighted when they're at a disadvantage, and when it comes to cash exchanges, we most certainly are. We can't tell the difference between a $10 bill and a $1 bill unless we're told. If someone wants to tell us the wrong thing, then we're thwarted. Again, I respect the consumer group's views on a lot of different subjects, and I do agree with the concept of total equality between the blind and sighted as an ideal to strive for. But I also feel that if the blind were able to identify all of their own money without depending on the sighted, then that would be a major step toward independence for the blind.

I know that there are products on the market that help a blind person identify their bills by speaking the denomination when you insert the bill in the slot.

Although this device has come down in price in recent years, and I myself now own one, most adaptive products for the blind are very costly, as I'll discuss in more detail in Chapter 8. Many blind people, because they're on fixed incomes, can't afford them.

Therefore, I hope that someday there are different sizes of paper money for everyone in this country. I believe that this would benefit all of us, both blind and sighted, and it would eliminate the need for paper money identifiers.

Chapter 8
Adaptive Technology for the Blind Can Be Costly

There are a great many adaptive products on the market that help the blind live more independently than they would be able to otherwise. The problem is that many of these products are too costly for those who are on fixed incomes. I would assume that out of the 70 percent of the blind in this country who are unemployed, many are on some form of subsidy, such as Supplemental Security Income (SSI). However, SSI provides only a very modest income. The maximum allowable payment to an individual in 2013 is $710 a month.

When I judge the cost of many of these adaptive products, I base my judgment on the standard pocket calculator. We all know what makes a calculator work. It needs a microchip that acts like the brain, because it calculates square roots, scientific notation, logarithms, percentages, exponents, etc., as well as the four main mathematical functions that we all learn as children. Yet the cost of such a calculator now averages between $5 and $10.

The traditional Braille writer that blind people use to write Braille is simply a mechanical device with seven keys, a carriage return, and a roller to roll the paper in and out. There are no electronic microchips in it. The functions are performed by hand, using these levers. I doubt that you would need any technical knowledge to build a standard Braille machine.

Nevertheless, the cost of a new Braille writer is $700. To put it another way, a blind person has to spend nearly his entire monthly SSI check in order to learn Braille the way I did, leaving him with no money for rent, utilities, food, clothing, and other necessities of life. In my opinion, a Braille writer should cost somewhere around $15, yet companies get away with selling this machine at the ridiculous price of $700, and I'm sure the cost will go up eventually.

If sighted people want to measure things around the house, they simply go to their local discount or hardware store and purchase a small measuring tape to do the job. I would assume that this item costs just a few dollars. I, too, would like to measure things in my apartment. However, as a blind individual, I would need to buy something that could adapt to my needs. The good news is that there is such an item on the market, and in fact, I own it. It's a talking measuring tape, which is about the size of a transistor radio. It comes in a leather case that zips shut when the tape is not being used. It measures in feet, inches, and the metric system. It performs far fewer tasks than the average pocket calculator does. Yet, if I need this talking measuring tape to help me live as independently as the sighted, I have to pay over $100 for it.

Why are these products for the blind so expensive? Some say it's because the demand doesn't meet the supply. But that still doesn't excuse the reality that a blind person on a fixed income can't afford to pay these absurd prices.

Let's take this a step further and compare computer items for the sighted and blind.

A sighted person can buy a hand–held, multi–task machine that acts as an address book, a notebook, and God knows what else for a very low price. The blind have a similar item called the Braille–and–Speak. It does all the same things as the sighted person's pocket computer; however, it's slightly bigger and includes speech software. The cost of the Braille–and–Speak is $1,400.

There's a product called the I.D. Mate, which scans bar codes and labels for blind shoppers. It is portable and quite helpful, but it costs $1,600.

JAWS, which is the screen–reading, text–to–speech software that many blind people use, sells for $1,100.

When you take a look at these items and compare them with the small calculators for the sighted, and if you stop to think about it, you have to ask yourself: Are the products for the blind really that much more sophisticated than products for the sighted are? I don't think the difference is so large that a blind person should have to spend so very much more than a sighted person does to have the same things done for them.

I think the blind are victims of something we learn about in economics, supply and demand. The blind are a limited market, which makes their products cost more—often far more. If I thought for one minute that these adaptive products were worth these outrageous retail prices, I would try to accept the situation. Yet, when we see the tremendous amount of brain power and simulated thinking that a lot of gadgets perform for sighted people at such a very low cost, and compare them with items for the blind that do half the work, you have to argue with the market. Why should a talking tape measure perform far fewer functions than a sighted person's pocket calculator with scientific notation, yet cost more than 10 times as much?

Does the problem lie with the manufacturer? Is it the wholesaler? Why can't they realize that you can't sell a $1,000 product to someone who makes $710 a month? Whoever is responsible for this situation needs to understand that the majority of blind people live on extremely limited incomes, well into the poverty category.

We need to put the blind on an even playing field, to help them live more independently. A major step in that direction would be to make adaptive products far more affordable than they are now.

Chapter 9
Self–Esteem

As you've no doubt gathered by now, I've spent a lot of quality time throughout my life with blind people. I was in school with blind children, lived with blind teenagers for years, have reunited with these same individuals many times as an adult, and have met other blind adults through my involvement in consumer organizations. Some of the blind people I know are very successful. They have good jobs, successful marriages, wonderful children, and a great outlook on life.

Yet, other blind people, more than I wish to acknowledge, are not very successful at all in one or more of these areas. Unfortunately, in some cases, they try very hard indeed, but still can't achieve success. As this book has already made clear, it's not as easy for a blind person to achieve success as it should be. In the thousands of conversations I've had with the blind over the years, I find that many of them have given up on their original goals. They seem depressed, apathetic, and lost.

As I implied at the beginning of this chapter, I knew many of these individuals as children, and their attitudes about life were positive back then. It doesn't take a rocket scientist to figure out what happened. When blind people reach adulthood, they start looking for jobs, relationships, and a sense of belonging. For those who appear depressed and apathetic, I believe the reasons lie with the constant rejections they face day after day. I'd like to think that I can rise above these rejections. God knows I've been turned down numerous times by employers throughout my life; I know it's because I'm blind. Many prospective employers don't know how to accept what they think is the challenge of hiring me. I use my frustrations and channel them into other paths, toward positive goals, because I have a tremendous drive to remain productive. On the other hand, others may have problems dealing with such putdowns.

Several of my close blind friends live their lives by listening to a radio or TV set all day, not knowing what's going to happen tomorrow. Every time I ask if they're looking for work, the answers get more repetitious with each inquiry, and the frustration becomes more evident as they speak of their futile attempts at being successful. Not only does work elude them, but assistance, too, is hard to pin down.

One blind friend of mine is a graduate of Perkins, the same school for the blind that I attended. He went on to college and received a degree in journalism. I'm assuming that he went to college right after high school. As of this writing, the man is 56 years old and has never had a job. How many sighted people of his age do you know in 2013 that can make that claim? This blind guy *tried* to go to work. He was trained in office procedures, communications, telephone work, typing, writing, etc. I would assume that most of his training took place during his high school years, when he probably had a lot of confidence about his future. Now, the most productive thing he does is go to the local YMCA to make sure he stays healthy in his fifties. To assist him personally, this man has his mail read to him once a month by a volunteer he applied for through an agency. For the rest of each month, the mail simply piles up and doesn't get read.

Another gentleman spent time in a sight–saving class with me in my home town when we were eight and 10 years old. He was a happy kid, and everyone loved him. I met him again at the junior college I attended. He was there, too, taking a few courses. I was very happy to learn that he played the accordion. It appeared at the time that this young man's future was bright. We all assumed that he would be successful at something he took up in college, or perhaps he'd have a successful music career.

In 2007, when I was writing the first edition of this book, I contacted this individual, who was then approximately 46 years old. It had been some 25 years since I had seen him in college.

It didn't take long for me to figure out what he'd been doing with his life, based on the tone of his voice. I asked him anyway. The man, who is visually impaired, was spending his days hanging around the house doing nothing. He had no job, and he'd given up the accordion. My guess is that it was his vision loss that had prevented him from being successful, for whatever reason. He was depressed and couldn't seem to channel his frustrations into a positive outlook on life.

I used to run a support group for visually impaired individuals with self–esteem issues. I invited my friend to join, because I felt he'd benefit from being around other people with similar issues, who would share problems and solutions with one another. Keep in mind that my friend admittedly spent his life hanging around the house. But when I invited him to join my support group, he told me he was too busy to go. It sounded to me that he was subconsciously looking for reasons not to do anything new, simply because he didn't really believe he would suddenly become a success, no matter what we might advise or suggest.

About 15 years ago, I hosted a local television show about disabilities. I would interview people in the medical profession, agency representatives, people with disabilities, advocates, business people, and presidents of consumer organizations. Each week, I would bring a guest on the show to talk about an important topic pertaining to blindness, deafness, or other disabilities.

One day I decided to ask a blind couple to appear on the show, so that they could explain how it's no big deal for blind people to raise their own children. At that time, the couple's little girl was five years old, and sighted. When I asked the couple to appear on my show, the mother became very anxious and insisted that I not ask them. It wasn't that they couldn't handle being in front of a camera. It wasn't because she didn't know how to talk so publicly about their relationship and their daughter. The mother was afraid that if her family's life story was aired on television, someone would be at their home the next day trying to take their daughter away from them.

I want to make it clear that the little girl is their natural born child, whose parents do a remarkable job with her and love her dearly. Under the circumstances, I asked the blind mother why she believed that someone would take her child away from her the moment their story appeared on television. I should have anticipated the answer, because it was so obvious. The parents, although they are caring, loving, and responsible, are BLIND! The mother was convinced that even though the little girl is her natural child, some social worker would find a way to break up the family by placing the child in a sighted environment.

Chapter 10
Legislation and Lobbying

Particularly in the last century, in order for the blind to be given opportunities equal to those of the sighted, several consumer groups, lobbyists, and private citizens filed legislation. In some cases, the blind themselves fought for extra benefits to supplement their limited incomes.

I want to begin this discussion by talking about the guide dog. In case you're not aware, a guide dog is allowed in a restaurant, on an airplane, at a bus station, and at any other public location that a blind person needs to be, because this particular type of dog aids the blind in travel. In fact, if a blind person lives in an apartment or other rented facility where the landlord does not allow dogs, the blind tenant has the right to own a guide dog and keep it in his home as a travel aid. That's the law.

Earlier in this chapter, I referred to how lobbyists have fought for extra benefits for blind people in recent decades, because it was recognized that the average blind person's income is extremely low. One example I can give regards bus service in my home town. A local politician, who was legally blind, once filed legislation which would allow a blind person to ride buses free of charge. All a blind person would need to do was to show the driver a pass, and he would be allowed on the bus without paying.

I used to take a lot of buses to and from college, and so at first, I felt privileged to be the recipient of such a benefit. However, as I became more involved with consumer groups and coalitions, I met people with other disabilities who also rode these same buses but had to pay for their rides. As much as I was grateful on behalf of other blind people for free bus rides, I found it rather unfair that people in wheelchairs paid for their bus rides while I didn't have to. Along with the blind, many people in wheelchairs find it difficult to obtain jobs. Therefore, understandably, their incomes are typically limited as well. However, they had no legislation concerning buses to help them.

One day I asked an agency director why the blind had managed to get free bus rides while passengers with other disabilities couldn't. In this executive director's opinion, the blind were better at lobbying and had more support. I don't know if that's true or not, but if it is, then why can't we find enough advocates to help us sell our skills when we're trying to find gainful and productive employment? Here in 2013, it seems to be just as hard for the blind to get a job as it was 50 years ago. Maybe we know how to get a free bus ride, but the large majority of us still can't seem to succeed in finding employment. I know there are exceptions, because I do know several very successful blind people, but the employment situation remains very bleak for far too many of us.

In 1994, our local bus company discontinued the free bus rides for blind passengers, partly because of the Americans with Disabilities Act. After all, if the ADA promotes equal treatment for persons with and without a disability, then the reasoning was that all persons with disabilities should pay the same prices as those without them. At first, I tried to fight the discontinuance of the free bus ride, but then I remembered just how unfair it was for passengers with other disabilities to pay while the blind didn't. At that point I began to accept the discontinuance gracefully and was proud to pay for my bus ride.

The seating arrangements on airplanes is another issue for which the blind have lobbied. More often than I care to admit, the blind have been asked to move from exit row seats on airplanes because it's believed that they can't handle an emergency situation. Like many other situations in life, there are some blind individuals who can handle such emergencies, while some sighted people can't, for whatever reason. There are also blind people who will admit that they wouldn't be able to handle a flight emergency, but they will do their best to defend a blind person's right to sit in an exit row seat if he or she chooses to do so.

While the blind have all this legislation on the books to assist them, there are those who choose to abuse the legislation to the point where they're willing to bend the rules for us, just because we're blind. I'll give two examples of this that I've had to deal with.

Blind people cannot qualify for supplemental security income (SSI) if they have too much money in the bank. In order to apply, we must go through a rather lengthy in-take process to determine eligibility. Yet, there are those who are so concerned about us blind individuals that they will do what they can, and say what they want, in order to make the point that we should get everything that's coming to us.

I have never qualified for SSI, yet I know people who were willing to take money out of my bank account and hide it in an escrow account so I could receive SSI. After all, they said, SSI is money for the blind. So, in their view, I deserved it no matter what. Even though I kept insisting that this would be dishonest, my so-called supporters said that they'd rather see me get the money than have some crook abuse the system. How ironic! Isn't that what these people were asking me to be, a crook? They were asking *me* to abuse the system. What kind of lobbying is that?

The postal system allows for certain packages to be mailed free if they're meant for a blind person. I don't know if I necessarily agree with this law, especially if it doesn't exist for people with other disabilities. It's similar to what I mentioned above, the former free bus ride. Nevertheless, the law exists, and I understand the guidelines.

Not too long ago, a man in my city told a friend of mine that he was going to prove that if I could become a certified blind customer in the eyes of the postal system, I could send out any correspondence without a postage stamp. In other words, I wouldn't have to put stamps on my phone bills, gas bills, résumés, or any other written correspondence just because I'm blind. All I would have to do would be to show the postal worker a certificate of blindness, and I would be exempt from putting stamps on envelopes.

This is a myth; there is no such exemption. But the myth comes from people whom you really have to forgive, because they don't know any better. All they know is that they have sympathy for the blind, and they really believe that our benefits should go as far as we can extend them. The truth is that even if the postmaster had a certified document proving that I'm blind, it wouldn't exempt me from anything. And what if I were to decide not to put my name on the envelope, just my return address? How would I prove to the postmaster that I was the one mailing it out, versus someone else in my household?

In short: As a blind citizen, I will use legislation wisely, not abuse it.

Chapter 11
The Blind: Victims of Circumstance

Several years ago, I was hired by a car dealership to order car parts and handle customer inquiries on the computer. During my time on the job, computer engineers appeared at the work site to determine whether it could be adapted properly for a blind person.

One day, after waiting a year for training, while I was sitting behind my desk at my job, I received a visit from my vocational counselor, a person who was with my local support agency. She had received a written report of a meeting that had taken place with the regional engineer from the agency, a contracted engineering consultant, and one of my bosses. The purpose of the meeting was to discuss adaptations for my job. The report wasn't very positive. Apparently, there was nothing that could be done to adapt a speech system so as to make it compatible with the Quick Books or All Data programs used by car dealerships.

Regarding the job itself, I was told to think positive despite the agency's findings. There might be some manual steps to be taken which would require my boss to talk into a dictating machine. However, those specific programs could not be adapted to speech systems.

Before there is any misunderstanding, let me clearly state that I blame no one at the agency or my bosses for this problem. If there isn't any way to adapt Quick Books or All Data for a blind person, then I can't hold any one person or agency responsible. In fact, I have called several computer software companies across the country, and they have pretty much confirmed the agency's findings.

I know that the blind are encouraged to call software companies if the agencies can't help. However, while talking to these companies, I more or less have to be a computer engineer in order to speak their language. I can honestly say that I know nothing about the mechanics of high–tech software. I'm just a consumer. When I'm on the phone with these companies, they ask questions that require knowledge of the mechanics. It's almost like my going to a brain surgeon for help and he asks me if my cerebrum and my medulla oblongata are functioning properly.

Having said all that, there was still the issue of my keeping busy all day while at my job. Though I know I can't speak for all sighted people, I'm sure that most of them would like to be busy throughout their work day instead of listening to a radio while waiting for the phone to ring. The blind population feels the same way. They want to be both needed and productive. My bosses would have liked it if I had kept busy, not only because it would have made me feel better psychologically, but because I was an employee. Employees are supposed to give their bosses productivity. When a boss hires someone, sighted or blind, he or she is making a financial investment, hoping that there will be favorable returns for the business.

Even though my bosses understood my situation, given that they had been my close friends for several years, I'm sure they hired me with a certain degree of expectation; otherwise, they would have hired someone else.

I suppose that if my bosses had wanted to have me sweep floors or wash cars, I might have been a bit more productive than I was in actuality. However, they knew that I was overqualified for that kind of work. When I was hired, I was given three titles: receptionist, parts manager, and office manager. As a result of my not being trained properly due to unforeseen circumstances, I felt that I was more of an expert on local politics, Boston sports, radio talk shows, rap music, and soap operas than I was on car parts.

What would you do, starting tomorrow, if you were faced with these problems?

After two long years without training, I was laid off from my job, and once again headed to the unemployment office. The one lesson that I learned from this experience is that the next time a boss offers training, I want to make sure that the training is in place before my first day on the job. I don't think that's too much to ask. Do you?

Despite all the time I've spent over the years being unemployed, I've led a very active life. Currently, I'm the editor of a consumer magazine, *The Consumer Vision*, which is read in more than half the states in the U.S. and on three other continents. In order to accommodate as many readers as possible, I make the magazine available in three different formats: Braille, email, and CD. I also write a weekly op–ed column in *Matilda Ziegler Magazine for the Blind*. During the fall and winter months, I run a bowling league which, for the most part, consists of bowlers with disabilities. Helping others makes me feel positive.

I know many blind people who knuckle under to constant rejection, and I don't know what to do about it. I'm doing my best not to let it affect me.

* * * * *

Editor's note:

This marks the end of the original text of *As I See It*, which was slightly modified and updated for this edition. The following chapters are additional, mainly short articles which were written between 2006 and 2013. Some of these articles were previously published by the author in *The Consumer Vision Magazine*, while others of them are appearing here for the first time. They cover a wide range of topics, including unemployment among the blind, various sports for the blind, the blind in relationships, technology that has proven either helpful or frustrating to the author, legislative issues and priorities, a potential problem with Grade 2 Braille, a tribute to the only blind director of Perkins School for the Blind, and much more. — Leonore Dvorkin

Chapter 12
Ignorance of our Abilities

Being blind, we know that part of our society regards us as stumbling, bumbling idiots. Not everyone looks at us that way, of course, but those who do probably either spent their entire life without coming into contact with a blind person, or they just drew their own conclusions anyway. What makes it more pathetic is when professional people see us as incompetent.

As I mentioned in Chapter 2, in 1984, I applied for a job as a telemarketer for a local newspaper. My visual disability did not stop me from making the effort, because I knew there were ways to accommodate me on the job. The interview started out okay, but then the employer asked me if I could dial a telephone. At that moment, the interview was finished as far as I was concerned. I could no longer conduct myself in a professional manner with this employer, nor did I have the same respect for him as before. I suppose I should have given him a pass, in case he had never seen a blind person dial a telephone, but the mere fact that he asked the question told me that he had doubts about how I could be a telemarketer, no matter how much effort I wanted to put forth. I told the employer that of course I knew how to dial a telephone. After all, I had called him to set up the interview.

The other day, I was sitting with a friend of mine who is legally blind. He received a telephone call from *The Boston Globe*, asking if he'd like to have their newspaper delivered to him. He respectfully told the woman that he is legally blind, therefore he wouldn't want the newspaper. Her response was, "Then how the hell did you answer the phone?" My friend, who's a bit more timid than I am, simply hung up on the woman and later expressed to me how insulted and offended he was by that remark.

It's one thing for someone off the street to ask us ridiculous questions about our capabilities, but when a professional does it, it brings the issue to a new level. Professional telemarketers or company presidents should not make remarks like that while performing a service to the public. If I had been on the phone with that telemarketer from *The Globe*, and if she had asked me how the hell I was able to answer the phone due to my blindness, I would have told her the following: "I put my hand on the receiver, lift it up gently, put the ear piece to my ear, the mouth piece to my mouth, and say hello." Then I would have slammed the phone down to show her I was capable of doing that, too, with no problem.

If you really want to know how we blind people do things, you may ask us, because maybe you really don't know. And this is why, for the most part, I can't really get mad at such comments.

Chapter 13
My Experience with Jury Duty

For years, blind people have fought for the right to sit on a jury. The common belief is that it would be difficult for a blind person to serve because he can't see evidence or facial expressions, making it hard to reach a fair conclusion. However, the lack of sight does not hinder our ability to make a fair decision. We can hear testimony and reactions, gauge attitudes, and consider other aspects of a court case. In short, we believe that we can be objective observers.

Practically ever since I've been old enough to vote, I've been receiving jury notices every three years. Despite my blindness, I not only believe that I can sit on a jury, but I would be proud to do so. I have listened to thousands of court cases over the years, both real and fictitious, so to me, the process in a court trial is easy to understand.

This year, when I received my jury summons, I was finally given the chance to actually be in the court. Usually when I call the jury information line on the business day prior to the date of my jury service, I'm told not to appear, because they don't need me. This year, things were different, and I went. On the specified day in July, I reported for jury duty at New Bedford Third District Court.

Even though court is in session beginning at 9:00 a.m., all potential jurors were asked to report an hour earlier. Apparently, they had summoned 18 people, but only 17 showed up. I don't know if the eighteenth person was ill, delinquent, or somewhere in between.

After waiting in the lobby for a few minutes, we were all escorted to a conference room, where we watched a 16–minute film about juries and trials. During that time, the court official who showed us the movie approached me and asked if I wanted to continue with the process. I suppose he felt that I could use my visual impairment as an excuse to leave. I told him that I wanted to stay, and he said he would speak to the judge about it. Apparently the judge then said it was up to me.

The group waited two more hours while all the cases were heard. If a case needed a jury, the entire group would have to go downstairs to a courtroom, where a jury of six would be hand–picked from among all 17 of us.

At 10:30, we were all summoned into the downstairs courtroom, because one of the civil cases required a jury. There was no agreement between the parties, so a jury was necessary. Before the judge picked six people to serve on the jury, he asked all 17 of us the same questions: Did we know any of the parties or witnesses? Did we have a prejudice regarding the situation before the start of the trial? And so on. The judge then picked six jurors. One of the jurors was rejected, so he picked a seventh. After the jury was seated, the rest of us went back upstairs and waited once again in the conference room.

At 12:15, the judge came into the conference room and told us we could leave, because all of the remaining cases had been decided one way or the other. The judge went on to tell us how powerful our presence was, because many defendants have a habit of asking for a jury trial as a means to delay their case, figuring that a jury trial would be rescheduled for a later date. If potential jurors are waiting, and if there are enough to form at least two separate juries, defendants can't play the waiting game, because jurors are already on stand-by.

You would be amazed at the number of people who tried to talk me out of jury duty. Many people wanted me to use my disability as a means to get out of it. I don't think it's necessary for me to get out of jury duty on account of my vision loss. I may not be able to see some of the evidence, but I'm a good listener and a good judge of the facts presented to me.

In fact, I did declare hardship when I was first notified, but it was only a transportation hardship, because they wanted me to go to Taunton. I switched to New Bedford because it was closer, but never once did I discuss my blindness, either in personal dialog or in written correspondence with the Court. I may have been bored out of my mind while I was waiting to serve, but I was proud to perform a civic duty that is required by our democracy. I would do it again, and if I don't get called in as an actual juror, so what? Along with everyone else who is summoned for jury duty, I have no way of knowing what's going to happen after I show up, ready and willing to be a juror. Once I'm there, the decisions are out of my hands. It depends on who the litigants are, what the cases are all about, and what's going to happen in those cases.

Chapter 14
The Unemployment Rate of the Blind:
A Shameful Lack of Progress

Thirty years ago, when I joined one of the two most popular consumer organizations for the blind in this country, I was told that the unemployment rate of the blind was 70 percent. After being with this particular consumer organization for a while, I assumed that the organization would work hard to try to lower that rate, because it's the organization's job to let the public know how the blind can lead independent lives. Despite my assumption, the unemployment rate of the blind today is still 70 percent, exactly the same as it was 30 years ago. In fact, some say it's gone up to 80 percent.

With all the accomplishments of these blind consumer organizations and other advocates who believe in what the blind can do, how can it be that the unemployment rate of the blind has stayed the same or even increased as time has gone by? It should be the other way around. More and more blind people should be joining the work force.

While I ask these consumer organizations why they have yet to lower this terrible statistic, I also have to consider other factors which contribute to the status quo of the unemployment rate of blind persons. Here in Massachusetts, our governor closed down a workshop that employed 25 blind workers. Prior to that, a well-known agency shut down its Braille program, resulting in the removal of a blind executive or two.

I realize how bad the economy is in general, so I don't expect the blind to find jobs that no one else can find. All I want and expect is for the blind and the sighted to be allowed to compete equally for available jobs. Given that the Americans with Disabilities Act was adopted in 1990 and then amended in 2008, and given the belief by the consumer organizations that the blind can compete on equal terms with the sighted in many job settings, I must ask the question again: Why the status quo in the blind work force? Why aren't the various State Commissions for the Blind working more closely with their clients to help them with self-advocacy? Why aren't these same Commissions doing more to sell their clients' skills to companies? Are they truly doing all that they can to try to convince companies that it's not a challenge to have a blind person on the job?

I would welcome some feedback regarding this topic. My email address is: **branco182@verizon.net**

Chapter 15
Another Perspective on the Unemployment Rate of the Blind

I've talked about some of the reasons why there is such a high unemployment rate among the blind community. I failed to mention another factor, one which I feel is a major contributor. That is, there are many blind people who are reluctant to get a job for fear that their disability check will be reduced. I can understand this fear, because one never knows how long a job is going to last and how long it would take that particular blind person to recover his lost benefits if he were to lose his job.

This is not a subject that I like to talk about, because I feel that it borders on intimidation by the system. Even though the blind are allowed to make more money by other means than persons with other disabilities are before their government checks are reduced, there is still a point where the blind person needs to worry about such a reduction in government benefits. I receive a government check, though it's based on my work history and is not about SSI, so as I become self–employed, I try to weigh all my options. If I knew that I could make a consistent amount of money each month, I could accept a reduction or a dismissal of my benefits, but I would have to make absolutely sure of the consistent flow of income first. After all, I, like anyone else, have to put food on the table, pay the rent, pay utilities, and do everything else possible to lead a normal life.

If I knew I could make an adequate amount of money, I wouldn't mind not receiving government benefits. Yet I understand why government benefits exist and what purpose they serve. Who, as a blind person, wouldn't get the concept? I've thought of ways that would give blind people more incentive to find work while on government assistance, and also for blind workers to have a smoother financial transition if, for whatever reason, they lose their jobs.

Here are my ideas. I think that the government should allow a certain grace period, during which a blind person could start a job, get paid, and still keep all government benefits for a designated length of time. The benefits would serve as a kind of insurance while the blind worker makes sure that he or she is secure in the job. I also firmly believe that an employer should be able and willing to step in if there is a later financial crisis (a necessary layoff, for example), in order to expedite the process with the government, so that the individual could begin receiving an adequate amount in benefits immediately.

Chapter 16
Trying to Make Ends Meet While Living with Physical Disabilities

On behalf of blind people, as well as others with physical disabilities who live on their own, I often wonder how we do it. I especially wonder how those of us who are on a fixed income or receive a government check manage to make ends meet, especially if the government check is all we get. I try to make ends meet without government assistance, but that's because I don't qualify for it. Aside from things like rent, utilities, and food, there are other expenses that sometimes come up in life—things that I would have difficulty with if I were getting only a government check.

Here's an example. Recently my bird needed to be seen by a doctor at an animal hospital, and the problem was so serious that they kept him overnight. It cost me nearly $300 for the entire process, as well as an additional $25 to have the bird taken there by car. Needless to say, these expenses were not in my budget. A week later, the bird had a follow-up visit; I had to pay an additional $25 for transportation plus approximately $50 for the doctor's visit. So here I've recently spent

$450 on a pet. To put it in perspective, the money I had to spend in order to keep my pet from being sick is over two-thirds of a monthly SSI check for most blind people—which, as I mentioned in Chapter 8, is a maximum of $710 a month here in 2013.

And speaking of transportation: I try very hard to keep up with my religious faith by attending church services, but how much money should I be expected to have to spend on transportation in order to please God?

Has anyone ever wondered how the government expects people on fixed incomes to take care of all their business like everyone else, given how much things cost? Some people may say, "Well, if you're on a fixed income, don't get a pet." Would these same people also ask us to stay home because transportation costs $25 per errand? Or would they also ask blind people not to have guide dogs, because the dog is an added expense, much as a regular dog is? If we're supposed to lead independent lives like everyone else, then please tell us how we can do everything the way we're supposed to and still stay within our budgets.

Last week I had a debate with someone on the phone who didn't think that younger people with disabilities should receive discounts, the way seniors do. If a young person with a disability isn't working, and if his income is equal to or less than that of an elderly person, why shouldn't he get a discount? How is he supposed to live without that kind of extra help? Many blind people own guide dogs. How do you suppose a blind person with a guide dog pays his rent, his grocery bill, his utility bill, his laundry bill, his transportation costs, and his bill for the care of his guide dog on a mere $710 a month, if that's what the government allows him to have? Please tell me, because I really want to know.

Chapter 17
Transportation Costs for Persons with Disabilities

I'm writing about a friend of mine who shall go nameless. He's in a wheelchair, on a fixed income, and doesn't go out very much because of circumstances I won't go into. As a result, the man is frustrated, because many times he wants to go out with his friends, but can't.

I invited my friend out to dinner with us at one of his favorite restaurants in Fall River, and of course he sincerely wants to go. The problem is, as is the case with many people in his situation, he can't find an accessible and affordable ride to and from the restaurant. I tried every means at my disposal to help him. Yesterday, I found a company that provides transportation. I called the owner and told her about my friend's situation. She asked if he could transfer his body into a regular car, and I said he could. In fact, it probably would be easier for him to do that because he can move his legs better than most other people in wheelchairs, who need an accessible van.

I thought I was having a great conversation with the owner of this transportation company. She was very sympathetic about my friend and wanted to take him to the restaurant. I gave her his address and the name of the restaurant, and then she quoted her price. As I said, my friend is on a fixed income. He doesn't work, and he makes just enough money to survive. Despite his limited finances, the owner of the transportation company wanted to charge him $80 for the ride to and from the restaurant. I realize that the restaurant is in Fall River, but I don't think that fully excuses the company. I can get to this same restaurant for $15, and I don't live too far from my friend.

For the record, I want to point out that this particular transportation provider is not the only company that charges these outrageous prices. There are numerous providers who have no problem telling a person with a physical disability to give them close to $100 of their limited monthly income in order to meet a social need. In other words, it's simple. Pay the $80 or stay home. What if we all had those limited choices? Could we survive socially?

I don't know how these transportation providers can sleep well at night, knowing what they charge people with disabilities who struggle to make ends meet every month. After all, we also have to pay rent, buy groceries, pay the utility bills, make medical co-payments, etc.

I've had numerous discussions with people over the years about this subject. I know all about insurance costs, operating costs, labor, and the like. Even though, as a businessman, I understand and respect everything that companies have to go through to be successful at what they do, I find it an injustice when a person with limitations, who wants to do the same things that the rest of us do, has to pay an outrageous amount of money that he doesn't even have in order to keep up.

Some of you may be asking about his family. Well, if he can't force his family to provide him with rides, then I can't comment or make that argument. Therefore, he, like everyone else in his situation, has to live with this terrible injustice. I'm tempted to ask a transportation provider what would happen if he himself had a loved one in a wheelchair who couldn't get out that easily, and then he had salt rubbed in the wound by being told he had to spend $80 to go out, and that doesn't even include his dinner.

I know that these transportation companies are private entities, and therefore, by definition, they can do what they want to do in order to compete with each other. Again, why does this all have to be at the expense of someone who not only has a limited income, but is physically limited? I honestly don't get it, and would like to hear someone try to justify it.

By the way, I know about the SRTA Bus Demand Response, which serves the disabled community in this area. (Their website is www.srtabus.com.) I use the service myself. However, the buses only run until 8:30 p.m. on weekdays, and the service hours are limited on weekends and holidays.

Chapter 18
Highway Robbery: Braille Watches vs. Talking Watches

A few years back, I offered to help a friend of mine locate a Braille watch for her father, who was losing his sight. I priced a standard man's Braille watch at a company in New York, and found that it cost $60.

Some of you know what a Braille watch looks like, but for those of you who don't, I can tell you that it's very similar to a regular wristwatch, only the cover opens up and you can feel the two hands. They've also added dots around the perimeter of the inside of the watch; those indicate the hours.

I think you could say there isn't that much difference between a sighted person's watch and that of a blind person. Yet if you look online for Braille watches, you will see that most of them now cost from $75 to $100. I would like someone to justify these prices. I've looked at Braille watches over the years, and I can't, for the life of me, understand why a blind person has to spend so much for something that really is a regular wristwatch with a few minor adaptations.

It all goes back to what I've always said about products for the blind. Companies are allowed to sell them at these ridiculous prices, but there's no real need for that. If I had the skills, I could take an average wristwatch, adjust the cover so that it could open and close, mark the perimeter with several small dots, and, voila!—a Braille watch. After these minor adjustments, am I supposed to be able to claim that the value of the watch went up to $75 or more? What did I do to it? What drastic changes did I make? The hands are still intact. The only difference now is that a blind person is able to feel them.

I told my friend that she would be much better off getting a talking watch for her father; she would save more than $50 in the process. That's because a quick online search will show you that most talking watches now cost between $6 and $20. Some announce the time in Spanish.

If you really want the best of both worlds and can afford it, there is one model from a company called Reizen that gives the user the choice of feeling the hands or listening to the watch say the time. That watch costs $69.95, with free shipping from MaxiAids.com.

I contend that a plain Braille watch should not cost many times more than a simple talking watch, when there aren't any microchips or circuits in the Braille watch. It's simple mechanics, like any other watch, with a little bit of refining.

There has to be a way to make these companies understand what they're doing to blind consumers, who, for the most part, cannot afford to be their customers.

All that being said, I would like to recommend MaxiAids.com, located in Farmingdale, New York, as a good source of adaptive products of many kinds, over 6,000 in all. Their main product categories include vision, hearing, mobility, medical, and computers. The company is owned and operated by individuals who are blind, deaf, and autistic. The MaxiAids catalog is available online, in print, and in CD-ROM format. Phone 1-631-752-0521 for information. The company also holds on-site training workshops for the blind, offering the blind marketable skills that they can use to attain gainful employment.

Chapter 19
Lobbying: What is the Role of State Commissions for the Blind?

I'm proud that we have a State Commission for the Blind in Massachusetts, and I believe that when lobbyists fought for an agency separating the blind from those with other disabilities, they meant well. It's not that persons with other disabilities don't need a supporting agency. Of course they do. However, many people in the disability community fear that if you lump the blind in with others with disabilities under the same agency umbrella, the blind will drop to the bottom of the barrel as far as support and attention are concerned. I don't know that for a fact, but I agree with this public fear. In fact, I know many people with other types of disabilities, especially those with developmental disabilities, who have jobs. But that's not true of the majority of blind people in this country, no matter how well educated they may be, or how hard they try to obtain jobs.

As a blind consumer, and as someone who wants to live as normal a life as possible, I have certain expectations of a Commission for the Blind which I feel are quite reasonable. While I don't think that Commissions for the Blind should figuratively hold our hands and guide us through life in every way possible, I feel that when we have obstacles put in front of us because we're blind, the Commissions should advocate for us more than they do. For example, if I go on a job interview, and if my potential employer refuses to offer me reasonable accommodation to help me on the job, I would much prefer that a powerful agency, which is responsible for knowing the laws, step in and help. While there are blind people with enough knowledge to be their own advocates, many are not trained to be—yet they have the same rights as those of us who are.

On one occasion, I was asked by a potential employer to describe the nature of the adaptive technology that would help me with my job. Because I knew I couldn't explain it to his satisfaction, I counted on the Commission for the Blind to explain it, because the Commission employs computer engineers in this field, people who know all there is to know about such technology.

If I decide to go for an extended period of job training at a company that will ultimately reward me with a job, either on their premises or here at home, I expect the Commission for the Blind to play a role in the process, especially where it comes to easing the employer's doubts in every way possible. Many employers will think of ways not to hire a blind person, and will exercise these ways in a manner where we can't prove they're practicing discrimination.

Commissions for the Blind have many professionals who can motivate employers to think outside the box by considering blind people for jobs.

Chapter 20
What Happened to Volunteerism?

I've said many times that it's now hard to find people to volunteer their time, whereas it used to be so easy. The reason could be that modern society is fast paced, with more and more people in the work force, therefore not having much free time to volunteer. However, after talking to a blind friend of mine recently, it really struck me just what a sad state of affairs we've reached.

My friend lives alone in a public housing unit, and he depends on volunteers to help him with his paperwork and to go through his mail. I won't mention who he is, because his name is not relevant to the story; only his situation is. What I'm about to tell you may shock you, but it's the truth.

This blind man is having so much trouble finding a volunteer that it's gotten to the point where his mail is read to him once a month. Yes, you read correctly: once a *month*. I don't think I have to tell you the impact of his situation. It's true that most of us receive a lot of mail that can wait a month or more to be read, but in a lot of cases, it can't wait that long. So do we sit back and accept my friend's situation for what it is, or do we come up with reasonable suggestions for a solution to his problem? I hate to think that there might be many other people in his situation who have to wait a whole month for their mail to be read to them, but what if it's true?

Let's go further with this. The only reason why my friend is lucky enough to have his mail read to him once a month is because he happens to have a volunteer who makes monthly visits to him for a couple of hours at a time. What if this volunteer didn't have time to visit him once a month? If that were the case, what in God's name would my blind friend do about his mail and the rest of his paperwork?

Friends, loved ones, and agencies serving the blind all try to encourage blind people to live as independently as possible, and they are absolutely right. However, as for reading the mail, it's not as easy as we think. Some people encourage the blind to go out and buy a scanner to read the mail. First of all, a good scanner is not cheap, and if you're on SSI, it might be impossible for you to afford one. Second of all, as you know, much of our mail is not typewritten, therefore the scanner won't read it anyway.

If I had my mail read to me only once a month, and knew I couldn't do anything to improve that situation, I'd worry every day that my gas, electric, telephone, and cable TV would be shut off, because no one would be telling me exactly when to pay the bills.

By this time, some of you are probably wondering where my friend's neighbors are, and why some of them can't read his mail to him. I can only tell you that he's a man of sound mind; therefore, I'm assuming he knows his desperate situation well enough that he has asked his neighbors to help him. I couldn't possibly picture a man of his capacity *not* asking for such a favor. But if his neighbors don't want to be bothered, there's nothing he can do about it.

In closing, I want to talk a little about my own efforts to obtain such a volunteer, someone to help me with routine business and paperwork. After waiting for eight years, I finally got one. That was not the agency's fault. It's a very good agency serving a lot of people, and it does its job very, very well. You can't blame an agency if no one wants to come forward and volunteer to read someone's mail to them and do a little paperwork for them for an hour or two a week. In the past, I was fortunate enough to have neighbors and friends who were willing to take a few minutes out of their busy days to make sure I was caught up with everything, and now I have the valued services of a volunteer. I hope this situation continues for me, and I hope my friend can eventually have a better situation for himself.

Chapter 21
A Personal Care Issue

In Massachusetts, there are at least two agencies that allow a client with a physical disability to take charge of his or her own personal care. The reason for this policy is to promote independence. I can understand that, because we, as people with disabilities, should try to lead as normal a life as possible. However, despite the efforts of these personal care agencies to allow us to be independent, I have major concerns.

Here's how this arrangement works. Once you're evaluated by these agencies, you're granted a certain number of hours a week for which your personal care attendant can work. The worker is hired by you exclusively, not by the agency. You conduct the interview and ask for references from the potential worker, if you choose to. Once a worker is hired, she fills out the time sheet every two weeks, you sign it, and then it's sent to the agency so that your worker can be paid.

On many occasions, things work out fine. The caregiver does her job properly and is paid based on the number of hours she works each week. She follows your rules, because you're the boss, not the agency. However, just because you're in the privacy of your own home, that doesn't protect you from bad things that might happen. The caregiver might turn out to be a thief, a drug addict, or an alcoholic, and then you, and only you, would be forced to make a very difficult and important choice. It's also important to note that if a caregiver breaks something in your home, you are liable for the damage, not the agency. The whole point is to put you in charge of your own environment.

In some cases, the client strikes up such a close friendship with the caregiver that the caregiver is allowed to overstep her boundaries. Some caregivers bring their little children to the job, and some bring their dogs. But please consider: With some rare exceptions, are employees permitted to bring their babies, their toddlers, or their dogs to other types of workplaces? Of course not, because there's far too much potential for serious disruption to worker productivity, property damage, and even injury to both the children and the adults.

Some caregivers leave the client in the middle of work to pick up their children from school, while on the client's time. Then there's the problem of caregivers who simply quit working without giving the client proper notice. I've even heard of a caregiver walking out on the job in the middle of bathing a client.

As you can see, there's a twofold problem with the policy that these agencies are trying to promote. The caregiver isn't liable for any damage or inconvenience, and the client, unless he takes full control, might well allow the caregiver to overstep her appropriate boundaries.

Once the time sheets are filled out, the money that the caregiver receives comes from the agency, and that particular money consists of our tax dollars. I for one do not want to run the risk of having my tax dollars spent for a situation in which a client is going to allow a caregiver to run personal errands on the client's time, bring her pet or child to the job, or walk out in the middle of the job.

I would much rather see an agency offer its own personal care attendants. That way, if there's a problem, all the client needs to do is call the agency, and the worker will quickly be replaced. Another good thing about workers who work directly for the agency is that they are most likely bonded. If a client is allowed to hire his own workers, especially if he puts an ad in the newspaper or on Craigslist, he really doesn't know what kind of worker he's getting, at least at first.

I know one thing. If, God forbid, I was so physically incapacitated that I needed personal care, I would never use one of those agencies that allow me to be the boss. I wouldn't want strangers in my house, and it wouldn't matter how good an interviewer I was. We're talking about my life and my property. All it would take would be one major hiring mistake on my part to lead to disaster. If I needed personal care, I would want an agency worker in my home, or a family member, or a close friend. Independence is great, but how far do you take it before you risk your own safety?

Perhaps in a more perfect world, I would not be opposed to agencies that allow the client to be the boss of his workers, but I think we all know better. There is too much crime and a lot of dishonesty, and there are not enough safeguards to allow that system to work all the time. While some clients have no problem under this system, others do. One of my friends had a personal care attendant walk out on him before she dressed him, because she "couldn't take it anymore." Being that he was the boss, he had to worry and wonder when another personal care attendant could take over. If the agency had hired the worker who walked out, they'd have sent someone else to the house to finish dressing him, thus avoiding any further stress or aggravation for the client.

Independence is fine, but safety is just as important.

Chapter 22
Handicapped Parking Law Is Not Foolproof

As you know, people who drive their own cars, yet have a disability, can use their placard to gain access to a handicapped parking space in front of a business. If you live in Massachusetts, have a disability, and are being driven, the driver can use your placard in order to park in that same handicapped spot.

But there's a loophole in the law—and unfortunately, there's not an easy solution to the problem created by it. That is, let's say you drive me to a store and I give you my placard to put on your windshield while you wait for me. If a police officer happens to question the legality of your display of the placard, how can you prove that I was ever in your car without the officer simply taking your word for it? For all the police know, you could have found a disabled person's placard in a dumpster or on a sidewalk, or you could have borrowed it a year ago, because the police only check your car, without bothering to find out where I am.

If you're not in the car, either, then it's worse. All the cops do is see a placard in your window, and without knowing if it belongs to you, to a relative of yours, or to no one at all, they conclude that you're not breaking the law. The police could be checking to see if you're legally parked in the handicapped space by seeing my picture on the placard, and meanwhile I could have found another ride home from the store, or maybe I wasn't with you in the first place. How would the police know for sure, even though you were totally honest in finding that handicapped parking place?

If you really stop to think about it, there's a lot of potential for abuse under these guidelines. That's because the police don't usually ask where the person with the disability is; they only want to know that if you're parked in a handicapped space, you have *someone's* placard on the windshield. They virtually never ask where the disabled person is, or how long he or she has been gone from the car.

In fact, as a quick check of online articles on the subject will reveal, abuse of placards for the disabled is quite widespread, and it costs larger cities hundreds and thousands of dollars every year in lost parking meter revenue. That's why I think that something different should be added to the laws regarding them that will help keep everybody honest.

Chapter 23
Accessibility to Websites for Blind Computer Users

Although there has been tremendous progress in recent years in making the Internet accessible to blind people, there are several things that we, as blind computer users, can't do. I know one or two blind individuals who use Craigslist, Facebook, and other related sites in order to network. The one problem we have is that we can't see the authentication verification code that pops up on the monitor when we log out.

As you probably know, this authentication verification code, which is a random list of letters and numbers, some backwards, slanted, or upside down, is designed to prevent hackers from remembering it, and that's why it changes with every attempt to log out. The problem is that a blind person can't verify it, because the speech software can't translate it. A sighted person has to be on hand at all times to dictate every new authentication verification code that comes up on the monitor, so that the blind person can verify it. Under these circumstances, how does a blind person manage to maneuver through these sites, where you have to post information by logging in and out?

I would like to be able to post ads on Craigslist without needing the help of a sighted person every time I log out, just so that person can read an authentication verification code that changes on the fly and is not understood by speech software.

Do any of you have any solutions? And if you're a blind user, how do you log out?

Chapter 24
Verizon and Its Limited Tech Support

If you thought that the Verizon Center for Persons with Disabilities would help a blind consumer with a major computer issue, think again. I've been having problems sending out my magazine because my Verizon server decided to tag it as spam material. When I called the Verizon office, a very nice woman answered the phone, and as I explained my problem to her, she tried to refer me back to tech support. I told her that being blind, I wasn't able to work well with tech support, and furthermore, neither tech support nor their supervisor admits any responsibility on behalf of Verizon for the problem. Despite what I told her, the woman could not help me any further because she didn't have the resources.

If Verizon has an office exclusively to assist consumers with disabilities, shouldn't they have some kind of accommodation process? Tech support people who work for Verizon do not know how to help blind people with computer issues because they aren't trained in adaptive methods. I feel that this office needs to be a bit more progressive if it's going to live up to its title.

Chapter 25
Slow Down, the Blind Need To Catch Up!

I am probably one of the most active blind people on Facebook. Thanks to a thoughtful lady in the Midwest who taught me over the telephone, I know how to find all recent Facebook postings, access Facebook group pages, look up other profiles which are public domain, send private messages, and post and share status updates. I currently navigate through Facebook using Mazilla Firefox 18.2, JAWS 8, and Windows XP.

Recently, the Facebook administrators decided to change the process, making it extremely difficult for me to update, post, and share my Facebook status reports with my current software. I was told to upgrade JAWS. However, in my case, the upgrade of JAWS comes with a tremendous penalty. I would have to get a new computer which will not have Windows XP and Outlook Express, because those two programs will no longer be supported. If I lose Outlook Express and Windows XP, it is believed that any replacements such as Gmail or Windows 7 won't be as accessible. So, it's damned if I do and damned if I don't.

Many blind people and those in the field of technical support believe that the software manufacturers who continue to update their products at a fast pace have little or no regard for how much or how little their products benefit the blind. The blind try like heck to prove they can compete on equal terms with the sighted, yet now there's a new obstacle in their path, the rapid change of high–tech products. I think I speak for most blind computer users when I express my total satisfaction with Outlook Express and Windows XP, because they serve my purpose. Currently, I run a nonprofit corporation, and a total upgrade or software replacement may potentially result in temporary disaster.

With all that said, I don't pretend to know a whole lot about this subject. I only have knowledge based on my own personal experience and from what others tell me. Therefore, I'm open to any suggestions as to how I can resolve my issues, as well as what we can do to work more closely with software manufacturers to make sure that the blind don't fall behind with these rapid product modifications.

Chapter 26
Paper Money Identifier Works Wonders

Now, here's a more positive aspect of technology.

For many years, I wanted to purchase a paper money identifier so that I could sort my own bills without the help of a sighted person. Like many other adaptive products for the blind, the paper money identifier was very expensive, and I couldn't spend that type of money while trying to make a living. Recently, however, the price of this product has come down, so I purchased it. I'm pleased to tell everybody how great it is for me to be able to identify my own money now. It's a wonderful feeling, and it makes me feel even more independent.

For those of you who haven't seen the paper money identifier, here's a brief description of it. It's a rectangular device with a horizontal slot at the top. You take the bill that you want to identify and push it into the slot, with the bill held vertically. Once you believe that the bill is inserted properly in the slot, you press a button on the left side of the device. In seconds, a clear female voice will say a number, which is the dollar amount for that particular bill. The identifier is very simple to operate.

A paper money identifier does more than just make it easy for a blind person to count his money, to know what to hand to a clerk when paying, or to know what to leave on the table as a tip in a restaurant; it now allows the blind person to catch someone who is trying to scam him. If someone wants to borrow $5 from me, and I give him a $10 bill, he'd better give me back $5, because the money identifier will know if he's trying to give me less change than he should.

In the future, I will be sure to bring this product to any fundraisers that I run, in case I'm given the responsibility of collecting cash. Look out, scammers! We blind folks are now one step closer to nailing you.

Chapter 27
A Double Standard Concerning Swearing

I would like to take issue with something that keeps coming up in the rules offered by certain organizations for persons with disabilities. Allow me to start out by asking a question. I'm sure that many of you are familiar with bowling leagues. There are money leagues, men's leagues, senior leagues, junior leagues, co–ed leagues, etc. There may even be leagues for the left–handed, blue–eyed, or those with rosy–red cheeks; who knows? In a bowling league of this type, a non–handicapped league, have you ever heard it stated in their rules that you're not allowed to swear? Furthermore, does it ever say that if you're caught swearing three times, you're suspended from league activity?

Please don't misunderstand where this is going. I don't swear, and I don't like it when people use foul language in my presence, so this is not about me condoning swearing, because I don't. The point is that society works very hard to bring the message across to handicapped individuals that swearing is bad, but it doesn't bring the same message across to non-handicapped swearers as often.

I belonged to two separate bowling leagues for the handicapped where it was voted that the no–swearing clause be included in the rules. If it's so important to make sure that a handicapped individual understands that he can't swear, so much so that we have to write a rule about it, then why don't we apply the same rule to the average, non–disabled, hard–working Joe who swears?

Here is the dangerous precedent that we set, sometimes without knowing it. When we work for an integrated organization, that is, one which includes handicapped and non–handicapped people, we can't send the proper message about swearing if we don't enforce it on the non–handicapped the same as we do on the handicapped. I see this all the time in my bowling league. When a bowler with a disability swears, he or she is called on the carpet, but when a non–disabled bowler shouts out the "F" word, it almost goes unnoticed. What kind of message are we really sending to persons with disabilities about swearing if they see non–disabled people get away with it?

Two weeks ago, a bowler with a disability used the "F" word, and what she heard was, "Watch your language; that's not nice to say. There are kids around." Moments after she used the "F" word, a macho, able–bodied bowler in his late forties used the same "F" word, and there was nothing but silence from those around him. No one seemed inclined to reprimand him in any way. Mind you, this macho guy swears all the time. Everyone who knows him well has heard him swear thousands of times and probably accepts it, no doubt believing that you can't tell him anything.

Nonetheless, I sarcastically opened my mouth and said, "Kevin, you'd better watch your language; that wasn't very nice, and there are kids around." I had never said such a thing to him in all the years I've known him socially, but at that moment, I was making a point. This same guy who swears every minute has no problem telling the handicapped girl not to do it, but he turned around and did it. But did all the children who were around the handicapped girl suddenly disappear when this guy swore? Of course they didn't.

I don't like double standards, and this was one of the worst cases of double standards that I can recall witnessing.

I know that at times we need to enforce certain rules so that people with mental challenges can learn. I agree that in a handicapped organization such as a bowling league for these individuals, it should be in the rules that hitting is not allowed. I understand that, because violence may be a symptom of someone's particular mental challenge. In the non–handicapped or able–bodied world, we all understand that violence is wrong, but you never see it included in the operating rules of a money league, a senior league, or a construction–workers' league.

So how can we change these double standards?—if possible, of course.

Chapter 28
Let's Not Overdo It

First of all, I want to say that when it comes to the rights of persons with disabilities, I believe that I'm one of the strongest advocates around. However, I would also say that some people overdo it. Let me give you an example of what I mean by telling you about a past incident in my bowling league.

Before I explain what happened, let me describe how the bowling lanes are set up. There's a seating area in front of the lanes where people wait their turn to bowl. In order to bowl, you have to take one step up onto the lanes.

In our league, we have a woman in a wheelchair. The reason we allow her to bowl, aside from the obvious, is because the bowling establishment has an accessible ramp–like device with sliding rails available for her so that she can take the bowling ball, roll it down the ramp, and out into the lane.

The woman's provider, who is her constant defender, has the wheelchair placed on the second level where the lanes are, and while she's waiting for her turn, the wheelchair is placed between lanes. Being that the wheelchair is large, the bowlers who bowl in her area were complaining for weeks that they couldn't concentrate, because the wheelchair was in their way.

Eventually, the complaints escalated so badly that the provider was told to leave the woman's wheelchair in the seating area below where all the other bowlers were seated. Several of the able-bodied bowlers offered to help move the wheelchair up the step when it was her turn, which would solve the whole problem.

Well, the provider wouldn't have any of it. She said that it's not the woman's fault that she's in a wheelchair, and that all the other bowlers need to understand. Furthermore, the provider couldn't guarantee this kind of help moving the chair to and from the lanes every week, and said that the woman in the wheelchair doesn't need to hear all the bowlers say that she's in the way, especially where it's not her fault.

At one point, after several of us tried to talk the provider into leaving her client in the seating area, my assistant director threatened to stop all bowling in my lanes until the provider complied. Reluctantly, the provider complied, but told me that she will call a lawyer or a representative of the Americans with Disabilities Act, because she felt that her client was treated unfairly. I pointed out that we gave her the solution, which was no big deal, but she refused to hear me.

I may be wrong, but the provider strikes me as the type who will use disability rights as a weapon every time she thinks her client is wronged in any way. It may be embarrassing for the client to hear that she's in the way of other bowlers, but then again, if I decided to stand around in other people's way, even though I walk but can't see, I would be told about it directly, because I don't have a provider. I also told the provider that the rest of us sit in the seating area and don't stand on the lanes waiting to bowl, so why can't her client join us? All the provider said was that her client is in a wheelchair, so everyone has to understand.

Is this a case of taking disability rights too far? The danger in taking these rights too far is that the disabled population could then be regarded as wanting special treatment. This is why, if someone wants to use disability rights to defend groups or individuals with disabilities, they should do it wisely and when it's appropriate to do so.

If this particular provider wants to use the Americans with Disabilities Act to defend her client, she must keep in mind that you mustn't inconvenience others in the process. These rights require equal treatment among all of us, disabled or not, and furthermore, the bowling league has many individuals with disabilities in it, even though only one is in a chair.

Prior to this incident, the provider had taken issue with the bowling facility for not being totally accessible to wheelchair clients. In the first place, the building has a grandfather clause exempting the owners from spending the money to make this change, because the building is over 60 years old. Lately, the owners have spent some money putting in a ramp up to one of the entrances, but that's only because it's being done out of the goodness of their hearts, not because of a law.

Your thoughts are welcome.

Chapter 29
Not Everything That's Not to Your Taste Happens Because of a Disability

It's common knowledge that people with disabilities are often met with discrimination. Even though we hope that this problem will go away as the public comes to better understand what persons with disabilities can do, I still see how discrimination is expected by the disabled in almost every situation that comes up.

Some time back, I was planning a reunion of former students of Perkins School for the Blind. The restaurant was very nice, and the management was willing to offer us a private room for our party of 50. While I was speaking to the manager, he informed me that we couldn't order off the main menu, and that I should pick several choices from the menu for us to consider during the event. The reason why the manager asked me to do that was because he was afraid there would be a huge backlog in the kitchen if everyone in our party ordered off the main menu, combined with all the other orders from the public section of the restaurant. That would most likely create a very lengthy delay in service to our party, according to the manager.

When I informed my guests of this, one of them had the reaction I should have expected. The person felt that I was asked to make some limited choices because we're a blind group. If we were sighted, this person thought, the manager would surely figure out a way to let us order from the main menu.

Unfortunately, there are people who think that whenever something goes wrong in a blind group or something less than ideal happens to a blind individual, it's because of the disability. In this case, I don't see how the fact that we're a blind group had anything at all to do with the restaurant manager's concerns about a backlog of orders in the kitchen. I certainly won't repeat this accusation to him, because there's no real logic to it. What's the difference if 50 sighted people in one big group order off the main menu as opposed to 50 blind people? The food would be cooked by the exact same staff in the exact same kitchen, creating the exact same problem.

It's true that discrimination exists, but I think it's a dangerous precedent when we start to assume it. It may be that there is discrimination here, but I don't see it— no pun intended.

Chapter 30
The Blind in Relationships

I think it's common knowledge that when a sighted person searches for his or her mate, one of the most important things that he or she considers is how attractive the potential partner is. Why not? We all need to be presentable and appear proper, so in that regard, looks are very important.

A blind person does not have the advantage of being able to look at his or her potential mate. When someone with no vision searches for a partner, he or she takes personality into consideration exclusively. I believe that this is a trait that every one of us should consider, because it's the personality, more than looks, that contributes to a relationship. Kindness, thoughtfulness, compassion, and respect are all aspects of personality, and these are the factors that play the major role in the success or failure of a relationship.

When I search for my soul mate, I always consider personality, and I would do the same even if I had sight. Although looks can certainly contribute to desirability, it's what's inside that counts. As a blind man, thus someone who has to depend entirely on how a woman behaves in order to judge how attractive she is, I can only encourage others to follow my example, sight or no sight. When a woman shows you compassion and respect, it's not her cleavage talking. It's her inner beauty.

Chapter 31
Our Legislators and Their Priorities

Have you ever wondered why our legislators have a reputation of not helping their constituents as much as they should? I think part of the problem is that they spend too much time passing ridiculous laws, while they should be devoting their time to the more important issues in life.

Here in Massachusetts, a group of blind consumers has been trying to have legislation passed that will mandate the availability of talking pill bottles. I believe that this is something worthwhile, which will help the blind have better access to their prescribed medications and to the routine by which these medications are taken. While it's taking years for this legislation to go through, I hear about the most ridiculous laws being passed throughout this country in different states, and I wonder why.

Instead of worrying about important issues to help us live better, I'm hearing that it's illegal to put pretzels in bags in Philadelphia, that it's illegal to eat more than three sandwiches at a wake in Massachusetts, and that in Maine in 1939, a bill was introduced to make it illegal to put tomatoes in clam chowder. This was considered a "barbaric New York custom."

My question is: Do you really care about any of these issues?

With all the problems that the United States has to deal with, can our leaders please concentrate on what's best for our people, and not pass such stupid laws? Let's get our priorities straight. Blind consumers have gone out of their way to think of creative legislation that helps all of us. Talking pill bottles would make sense on all levels, especially for those who take numerous prescribed medications on a daily basis.

Chapter 32
Do Curb Cuts Affect Mobility Training?

Since the 1970's, when the blind were taught to search for the curb with their canes while trying to locate an intersection, legislation has changed drastically in favor of wheelchair pedestrians. While the blind must do their best to locate where the sidewalk ends and the street begins, cities and towns have been mandated to construct a curb cut at every street corner, allowing a person in a wheelchair to cross a street more easily. While I'm extremely grateful that wheelchair pedestrians have this support, I wonder how mobility instructors work around this reconstruction when teaching the blind how to cross a street. I've attempted to cross streets with curb cuts, and to be truthful, it's not an easy task.

We hear so much about other problems that blind people face on a regular basis, but seldom do we hear about mobility training. Have there been any major conflicts in the past 30 years between those who promote mobility training for the blind and those who promote curb cuts? I will assume, for the moment, that there have been no such conflicts, or I would have heard about them. With that said, I'd like to find out how mobility instructors have changed their curriculum to accommodate the wheelchair legislation.

You're probably wondering why I would find it difficult to locate a curb cut with a cane. I'm not implying that I would have difficulty with all curb cuts. If all curb cuts were designed in exactly the same way, according to the specifications mandated by law, then there would be no problem. However, some curb cuts are designed at a different slope than others, making it difficult to detect them with a cane. So some of us blind folks may think that we're simply walking down a slight hill, when in fact we're about to cross a street.

As always, I welcome any comments from readers on this issue. My email address is:
branco182@verizon.net

Chapter 33
Can Grade Two Braille Spell Trouble?

When Braille is taught, it's usually taught in steps. First, there's "Grade One" Braille, which consists of the entire Braille alphabet and some punctuation. As students of Braille become more advanced and proficient with the language, they're taught "Grade Two" Braille. Grade Two Braille offers a series of contractions, which most people would call a kind of shorthand. I suppose that the inventor of Braille decided to assign certain abbreviations to a series of words, and then those were taught to the blind. For example, each letter of the alphabet in Grade Two Braille, except for the letters A, I, and O, represents a whole word. The letter B stands for "but," the letter C stands for "can," etc. To get to the point of this article, I will now give you a letter that stands for a longer word. The letter K in Grade Two Braille stands for the word "knowledge."

Assuming that most blind children who learn Braille are in either first or second grade, many may be learning these Grade Two contractions and abbreviations before they learn how to spell the actual real word, as sighted children do. If you're blind, think back and try to remember. Did you know how to spell the word "knowledge" when you were six years old? If you learned Braille at age six, and you learned how to write the word knowledge by simply writing the letter K, chances are you'd never have to know how to spell "knowledge," unless you took up typing or word processing and needed to learn that word.

Grade Two Braille also offers different symbols for other words, such as "and," "for," "with," "the," and "of." Am I suggesting that little children didn't know how to spell these words before learning these shorter Braille versions? No, but I do know a 35–year–old Braille reader who spells the word "with" as "width." When I saw that in some of her correspondence recently, I couldn't help thinking about the possibility that learning Braille contractions at a very young age may keep some Braille users from ever learning the real spellings.

Here is one more example of my concern. Another feature of Grade Two Braille is abbreviated contractions. For example, the word "could" is taught as "cd"; the word "good" is taught as "gd"; and the word "your" is taught as "yr."

One day, a young blind boy was in a spelling class. He was about eight years old, and a very good Braille reader. The teacher asked him how to spell "good," and he answered, "gd." I'm sure you can imagine the look on the teacher's face when he spelled it that way. Yet, to the little boy's credit, he probably never knew how the word "good" was really spelled, because he had learned the Grade Two contraction in first grade, while all sighted first graders would have to learn the real spelling.

For my blind readers, I ask you: Am I making too much out of this? For my sighted readers, I have a suggestion. If you know a young blind child who's learning Braille, it may not be a bad idea for you to make sure that he or she learns the real words that Grade Two Braille contractions stand for—even if for no other reason than to avoid embarrassment as he or she gets older.

By the way, I have a confession to make. When I learned Braille at the age of eight, I did not know how to spell the word "knowledge" until after I learned the Braille contraction for that word.

Chapter 34
Beep Baseball: Adaptive Baseball for the Blind

When I was at Perkins School for the Blind, I participated in several sports, including bowling and baseball. Back in the mid–1970's, baseball was just beginning to be adapted for the blind, so the children at Perkins played regular baseball. The pitcher would throw the ball to home plate on a bounce, and as soon as the batter heard the bounce, he swung. When the player ran the bases, he would be called to the next base if he couldn't see where he was going. I felt at the time that the game was well suited for someone blind or visually impaired, because of all the assistance we received from our teammates and the staff members.

Under those circumstances, I would feel the same way today about regular baseball, if it were still being played by the blind. However, a new form of baseball, called Beep Ball, was invented exclusively for the blind.

Here is a very brief history of the sport, courtesy of the Wichita Beep Baseball Association.

Charley Fairbanks, an engineer with Mountain Bell Telephone, invented a beeping baseball way back in

1964. In 1975, the Minnesota Telephone Pioneers presented John Ross, Director of the Braille Sports Foundation, with a ball that had a better sound module and was better able to stand up to the crack of a solid bat. It was not long afterwards that the game of competitive Beep Baseball, or just Beep Ball, was born.

The game is similar to regular baseball in some ways, but it also has different rules, which are designed to make the game more convenient for blind participants. First of all, the ball is slightly bigger than a regular baseball, and when it's not in use, it has a wooden pin inserted inside. When the ball is ready for use, the pin is removed, allowing the ball to release a loud, continuous beeping sound. With this sound, everyone in the game has a good idea of where it is. As the ball continues to beep, fielders can locate it, and the batter knows when it's being thrown by the pitcher, giving him an opportunity to hit it.

In Beep Ball, players do not run the bases the way they do in regular baseball. There are two bases, one where third base normally is, and one where first base normally is. Each base makes a sound, and someone will activate it when the ball is hit. If the ball is hit toward third, the base is activated, and the base runner heads there. If the ball is hit toward first, then the runner heads for that sound. The object of the game is to reach your base, whichever one it is, before a fielder finds the ball. If you successfully reach base, a run scores, and you then go back to your bench. The game has fewer rules than regular baseball. In other words, there are six fielders, and all they have to do is position themselves around the field to find the ball before a batter reaches his destination. If the fielder locates the ball first, it's an out. There are still three outs in an inning of Beep Ball.

In 2001, I had the pleasure of managing a Beep Ball team in New Bedford, and we played a few games against other teams throughout the state. I found it to be quite a learning experience, although not terribly difficult. In case you didn't know, Beep Ball has its own World Series, so it's quite organized.

We should be grateful that many sports are adaptable for persons with disabilities, allowing us a chance to develop our physical skills and have a lot of fun into the bargain.

Chapter 35
Former Perkins School Director Remembered

In 2008, I was quite saddened to hear that Benjamin Smith, former director of the Perkins School for the Blind, had passed away on August 7 of that year. He was 95 years old. According to an August 17, 2008 article on him in *The Boston Globe,* Mr. Smith died of complications from a heart condition. But at least he had lived a very long and productive life. He was at Perkins for a total of 38 years, first as a teacher and then as an administrator, retiring from there in 1977.

I credit him with being the director who brought many changes to Perkins, whereas up to then, students had lived by very strict rules on the campus. I was one of the fortunate students who were at Perkins throughout Mr. Smith's entire term as director, so I was a witness to all that he did. He served in that role from 1971 to 1977 and was the only blind director Perkins ever had.

Prior to Mr. Smith's role as director, punitive action would be taken against boys and girls for showing affection toward one another. Quite often, students were given a three–day suspension if they were caught kissing. In the second year of Mr. Smith's term, the rules regarding interaction between boys and girls were relaxed some, given that he introduced what was known as cottage dating.

The cottages on the campus are similar to college dorms, in that students live in the cottages if they can't go home. With cottage dating, students at Perkins could go to other cottages to visit their girlfriends and boyfriends there. When cottage dating was first instituted, I was quite impressed with the concept. Yet I found it rather strange, because I never thought any Perkins director would take such a liberal step. When a boy finished visiting his girlfriend at her cottage, he would go back to his cottage by himself. However, when a girl finished visiting her boyfriend at his cottage, the boy had to accompany the girl back to her cottage and then go back to his.

Mr. Smith also introduced the independent living program, and he included several courses in the Upper School curriculum toward that end. In fact, several students became so independent that they were given their own keys to the cottage. I don't think this ever happened prior to 1970; the school was too strict for that.

As many of the academic students were leaving Perkins for various reasons, Mr. Smith went in a different direction, by bringing in more students with special needs. At the same time, many of the Upper School cottages became co–ed. Bridgeman and

Tompkins, which were once cottages for junior high and high school boys, were now young adult cottages, consisting mostly of adult men and women: either those who had graduated from Perkins and needed additional independent living training, or new clients who were brought to the school for this type of training. Brooks and Fisher, which had been cottages for junior high and high school girls, were now co-ed cottages for undergraduates, including those in either the B or U divisions.

By the time I graduated in 1977, which was also Mr. Smith's last year as director, every Upper School cottage except May and Moulton was co-ed, meaning that girls and boys lived under the same roof. After all those years during which a student could be suspended for kissing a classmate, does anyone really think that nothing more daring ever went on in these co-ed cottages?

Even though he loosened a lot of the rules that Dr. Waterhouse and his predecessors had enforced, Mr. Smith had strict morals of his own. One afternoon during my sophomore year, he called the entire Upper School student body into the chapel and gave us a talk about why it isn't nice to swear. At that time, many students were swearing a lot, and I guess Mr. Smith had gotten wind of it.

On a cool Friday afternoon in 1975, I was summoned from my typing class and was asked to appear in Mr. Smith's office. My father was there presenting Mr. Smith with a check for $1,500. My father owned a night club and had decided to hold a fundraiser for Perkins, with several bands donating their time. He explained to Mr. Smith that the check was not made out to Perkins School, but to the "Children of Perkins School." My father didn't want any of the money raised to go toward administrative costs. He wanted to make sure that every penny went toward the education of the children.

Another big change that took place under Mr. Smith's direction had to do with gym classes. Previously, boys and girls had taken gym separately. Mr. Smith made gym classes co-ed. As was the case with cottage dating, I was very impressed with this new concept of taking gym with girls, and frankly, I didn't mind. It's not as though we all took showers together. We just took gym class together.

I remember visiting Mr. Smith in his apartment with the rest of my graduating class. At that time, it was a tradition for seniors to visit the director the week of graduation. I can't speak for the others, but I know that I felt very honored to have the director of Perkins open his doors to us.

I believe that Mr. Smith will be remembered for taking a school that many thought was an institution and turning it into a school with a few contemporary touches.

The newspaper article referred to above appeared in *The Boston Globe* on August 17, 2008. The title is "Benjamin Smith, 95; lead [sic] the Perkins School for the Blind." The reporter was Bryan Marquard.

You can read more about Ben Smith, Perkins, and my eight years as a student there in my autobiographical book *My Home Away from Home: Life at Perkins School for the Blind*, which was published in 2013. It's available in both e–book and print from Amazon and numerous other online sellers, as well as in audio CD format directly from me. For ordering details, please see the section "Books by Robert T. Branco," which follows here.

Books by Robert T. Branco

My Home Away from Home: Life at Perkins School for the Blind

Autobiography / © 2013 / 200 pages

For details, see

http://www.dvorkin.com/robertbranco/

Available in both print and e-book formats from Amazon and other online sellers.

Paperback: $12.00 / E-book: $4.99

Also available in paperback or in audio CD format directly from the author for $16.00 ($12.00 for the book or CDs plus $4.00 for shipping and handling).

The CDs were produced by The Perkins Braille and Talking Book Library. The recording of the book consists of a total of six CDs, all for $16.00.

To order the CDs or the paperback from the author, please make out a check to Robert Branco for $16.00 and mail it to:

Bob Branco

359 Coggeshall St.

New Bedford, MA 02746

What We Love to Eat
© 2012

This cookbook is made up of recipes that were all submitted by blind contributors. It's available in three formats: large print, Braille, and audio CD. All sales benefit *The Consumer Vision Magazine.*

To order the book in any format, please make out a check to Robert Branco for $14.00 and mail it to him at the above address ($10.00 for the book plus $4.00 for shipping and handling).

As I See It: From a Blind Man's Perspective (the original, shorter edition) AuthorHouse, 2007

Now out of print.

As I See It: From a Blind Man's Perspective (Revised and Expanded Edition, 2013)

You can purchase paperback copies of this book online from sellers such as Amazon and Barnes and Noble or directly from the author. To order a copy from the author, please make out a check to Robert Branco for $14.00 ($10.00 for the book plus $4.00 for shipping and handling) and mail it to Bob at the above address.

Note: For now, the shipping and handling charge for the books and CDs is $4.00. This charge will be subject to change if mailing costs rise in the future. Ordering details will be kept up to date here: **http://www.dvorkin.com/robertbranco/**
You can also reach Bob by email at

branco182@verizon.net   or   by   phone   at 508–994–4972.